America in World History

Rise to Global Power
(1898 to 1965)
Volume 3

Volume 1

America as World Frontier (First Encounters to 1776)

Volume 2

America in the Age of Nation Building (1776 to 1898)

Volume 3

Rise to Global Power (1898 to 1965)

Volume 4

Challenges to Globalization (1965 to the Present)

AMERICA IN WORLD HISTORY

RISE TO GLOBAL POWER
(1898 TO 1965)
VOLUME 3

General Editor
Susan Crean

Consulting Editor
Tom Lansford
University of Southern Mississippi

SHARPE REFERENCE
an imprint of M.E. Sharpe, Inc.

SHARPE REFERENCE

Sharpe Reference is an imprint of M.E. Sharpe, Inc.
M.E. Sharpe, Inc.
80 Business Park Drive
Armonk, NY 10504
© 2010 BY M.E. SHARPE, INC.

Produced by
White-Thomson Publishing Ltd.

+44 (0) 845 362 8240
www.wtpub.co.uk

Editor: Susan Crean
Proofreader: Laurel Haines
Indexer: Jenny Caron
Text Design: Clare Nicholas and Bernard Higton
Map Design: Stefan Chabluk

Library of Congress Cataloging-in-Publication Data
Crean, Susan Rossi, 1970–
America in world history / Susan Crean, Tom Lansford.
p. cm.
Includes bibliographical references and index.
ISBN 978-0-7656-8171-3 (hardcover : alk. paper)
1. United States—History. 2. World history. I. Lansford, Tom. II. Title.
E178.C859 2010
973—dc22
2009015865

Printed and bound in Indonesia
The paper used in this publication meets the minimum requirements of
American National Standard for Information Sciences
Permanence of Paper for Printed Library Materials,
ANSI Z 39.48.1984.
(c) 10 9 8 7 6 5 4 3 2 1

Publisher: Myron E. Sharpe
Vice President and Director of New Product Development: Donna Sanzone
Executive Development Editor: Jeff Hacker
Image Researchers: Gina Misiroglu, Cathleen Prisco
Cover Designer: Jesse Sanchez

CONTENTS

New Immigration

From the late 1800s through the 1930s, a massive migration of people occurred around the world and resulted in the influx of millions of people into the United States—until restrictions limited their numbers.

During the nineteenth century, Europe underwent demographic and economic changes that encouraged emigration. Populations surged, particularly in southern and eastern Europe where, for example, the Italian population grew by 6 million from 1880 to 1910. This population growth contributed to the fragmentation of landholding, making it increasingly difficult for peasants to support themselves. At the same time, industrialization undermined enterprises such as weaving and products that peasants had previously made to supplement their incomes.

Responding to these pressures, approximately 100,000 people moved annually within Europe between the 1850s and 1880s, particularly to urban areas. From 1843 to 1900, for instance, Austria's urban population tripled. By 1900, however, slowing industrial development prevented Europe's cities from absorbing the population increase. With urbanization, ethnic tensions rose, including the reemergence of anti-Semitism after the stock market crash of 1873. Russian Jews also suffered violent czarist-encouraged pogroms from 1881 through 1884 and again from 1903 through 1906.

Political factors also contributed to instability and population movements around the world. The Philippines, for example, fought for independence against the Spanish beginning in 1896 and again against the United States from 1899 through 1903. Another example of political instability was the 1910 revolt in Mexico. The uprising was triggered when President Porfirio Díaz (1830–1915) left peasants virtually landless by transferring their farm holdings to a few large landowners, called *haciendados*, in the 1880s and 1890s. Political events in individual countries resulted in relatively small movements of people, especially in comparison to the politically driven migration of World War I (1914–1918). During that time, millions of people were displaced, including 1.75 million Armenians, some 600,000 of whom died, which Turkey had sent to Syria and Palestine.

Steamships took about 12 days from Great Britain and 20 days from Italy to sail across the Atlantic.

The Debate over Immigration

The effort to restrict immigration drew on an emerging body of racial theory, such as Arthur de Gobineau's (1816–1882) *Essay on the Inequality of Human Races* (1853–1855), which argued that the world was divided into three races: yellow, black, and white. Focusing on Europe, Houston Stewart Chamberlain's (1855–1927) *Foundations of the Nineteenth Century* (1899) viewed racial struggle as the driving force of history. Such theorizing influenced Madison Grant (1865–1937), a New York attorney whose best-selling book *The Passing of the Great Race* (1916) divided Europeans into three groups: Nordics, Alpines, and Mediterraneans. Grant's argument that only the Nordics could be assimilated into American society strongly influenced U.S. public opinion as Congress moved toward establishing the immigration quota system.

WORLDWIDE MIGRATION

Although Europeans emigrated in large numbers to Australia, New Zealand, and Canada, Latin America overall remained the most popular destination outside the United States until 1900. More than 100,000 Italians, for instance, moved to Brazil annually in the late 1880s and the 1890s. By 1907, Argentina had become more popular—with 78,000 Italian immigrants entering that year, compared with 21,000 going to Brazil. Besides becoming the dominant ethnic group in Singapore, Chinese laborers also emigrated to Latin America. Approximately 100,000 Chinese workers had arrived in Peru by 1875 and 130,000 in Cuba by 1873. After the abolition of slavery, more than 500,000 Indian contract laborers entered former slave colonies such as Mauritius and the British Caribbean, and 80,000 Indians arrived in the French Caribbean during the last half of the nineteenth century. Indians also migrated in large numbers to South Africa, Malaya, Singapore, and Fiji. Beginning with the Australian gold rush of 1851, Chinese, Japanese, and Filipinos entered that country in large numbers until exclusion was enacted in 1901.

U.S. IMMIGRATION

Amid these developments, individuals sought to improve their living standards. Although people were moving worldwide, American railroad, steamship, and industrial advertising of both transportation and jobs helped make the United States the most popular destination by 1900, especially for Europeans. As immigrants settled in the United States, they sent letters home that attracted more immigrants, a process that became known as chain migration.

Prior to 1890, European immigration to the United States was dominated by northern and western Europe in what historians have traditionally referred to as "Old Immigration." Between 1871 and 1890, more than 1.3 million immigrants arrived in the United States from Great Britain, more than 2.1 million from Germany, nearly 1.1 million from Ireland, and approximately 900,000 from Scandinavia. In contrast, fewer than 500,000 immigrants came to the United States from Italy or Austria-Hungary or Russia. After 1890, however, southern and eastern European immigration increased dramatically. From 1891 through 1900, 651,893 immigrants arrived from Italy, 592,707 from Austria-Hungary, and 505,290 from Russia, the latter mostly Jews. Immigrant numbers from these countries increased during the following decade, with Italy and Austria-Hungary each sending some 2.1 million immigrants and Russia sending more than 1.5 million. Even though World War I largely halted European immigration between 1914 and 1918, more than 1.1 million Italians entered the United States during the period from 1911 through 1920, while Austria-Hungary and Russia each sent approximately 900,000.

Immigrants arriving in New York went through Ellis Island after the federal government took control of immigration in 1892.

New Immigration

Since the 1920s, historians have often referred to the influx of southern and eastern Europeans as "New Immigration," but in recent years they have largely discarded this terminology for three main reasons. First, reference to New Immigration disguises the fact that northern and western European immigration, although declining in numbers, still constituted more than one-third of European immigrants between 1891 and 1920, with 1.1 million arriving from Britain, 1 million from Germany, more than 800,000 from Ireland, and another 800,000 from Scandinavia. Second, significant numbers of immigrants came from other parts of the world. Although the Chinese Exclusion Act (1882) sought to halt immigration from that country, approximately 35,000 Chinese entered the United States between 1891 and 1920. Nearly 240,000 Japanese arrived during the same period, and, although comparatively small, nearly 7,000 Indian immigrants arrived between 1901 and 1920. More than 25,000 Filipinos entered the United States during the same period, four-fifths of them into Hawaii. During those same two decades, immigration from Mexico also increased dramatically, with more than 49,000 arriving between 1901 and 1910 and 219,000 the following decade. The third main reason for discarding the term New Immigration is that it has become dated; still newer immigrant groups have arrived in the United States since the 1920s.

Impact of Southern and Eastern European Immigration

Southern and eastern European immigrants provided much of the labor force for American industry in the early 1900s. A study of 21 industries in 1910 found that 52 percent of workers were foreign-born, two-thirds of them in southern and eastern Europe. These immigrants contributed to the religious and cultural diversity of the United States by increasing the number of Catholics, establishing Orthodox Christian churches, and creating a major Jewish presence.

Russian Jews, who mostly arrived as families, settled in cities in the Northeast and Midwest, where they were concentrated in the garment trades and retail businesses. Because they were fleeing persecution, the Jews had a return rate of less than 5 percent between 1908 and 1924. During the same period, Italian immigrants, among whom males outnumbered females by three to one, established themselves along the northeastern seaboard. Primarily manual laborers, they often came to the United States expecting to earn money that would enable them to buy land back home in Italy; an estimated 54 percent of Italian immigrants during this period returned home. Hungarians, Poles, Croatians, and Slovenes settled in the industrial cities of the East and Midwest. They, too, were mostly men who expected their stay in the United States to be temporary. Between 1908 and 1924, more than half of them returned to Europe.

At Ellis Island, inspectors gave each immigrant a medical exam and checked their papers before releasing them to enter the United States.

Although they came to the United States in much smaller numbers, Chinese, Japanese, Mexican, and Filipino immigrants during the early twentieth century were predominantly male and settled mostly in the West, where they provided labor for mining, timber, railroads, and agriculture.

RESTRICTING IMMIGRATION

Believing that immigrants lowered wages and brought alien cultures into the country, some Americans began pushing for restrictions. Beginning with the Foran Act (1885), Congress passed laws prohibiting foreign contract labor, but there was little enforcement. The Immigration Act of 1891 transferred control of immigration from the states to the federal government, to be overseen by the Bureau of Immigration. It also established standards for the physical and mental condition of immigrants. Meanwhile, pressure groups had emerged and pushed for limits on immigrants, particularly the anti-Catholic American Protective Association (1887) and the Immigration Restriction League (1894). Beginning in 1897, Congress passed a literacy test requirement for immigrants three times, only to have it vetoed by three presidents—Grover Cleveland (1837–1908), William Howard Taft (1857–1930), and Woodrow Wilson (1856–1924). In February 1917, Congress passed the Immigration Act, overriding President Wilson's previous veto. It barred people aged 16 and older who were illiterate from immigrating to the United States.

The outbreak of World War I greatly reduced the number of European immigrants coming to the United States; fewer than 150,000 arrived between July 1, 1915, and June 30, 1916. When the war was over, immigration picked up again, with about 430,000 Europeans coming to the United States in 1919 and 1920. Restriction efforts continued during this time, however, stimulated by the fear of communism that gripped the United States during the Red Scare of the 1920s.

Through the Emergency Quota Act (1921) and the National Origins Act (1924), Congress severely limited the total number of immigrants the country would allow in from outside the Western Hemisphere and established quotas by country of origin. The latter legislation based quotas on the 1890 U.S. census, thereby severely limiting the number of southern and eastern European immigrants and effectively banning the Japanese altogether. The era of open immigration had ended.

Gary Land

THE UNITED STATES, A "WORLD FEDERATION"

Amid the clamor for immigration restriction, journalist Randolph Bourne (1886–1918) wrote in the July 1916 issue of *The Atlantic Monthly* that a new "transnational" United States had already emerged and should be celebrated. Anticipating the multiculturalism of the late twentieth century, he wrote:

"In a world which has dreamed of internationalism, we find that we have all unawares been building up the first international nation. … America is already the world-federation in miniature, the continent where for the first time in history has been achieved that miracle of hope, the peaceful living side by side, with character substantially preserved, of the most heterogeneous peoples under the sun."

GUIDED READING

Daniels, Roger. *Coming to America: A History of Immigration and Ethnicity in American Life.* New York: HarperCollins, 1990.

_____. *Guarding the Golden Door: American Immigration Policy and Immigrants Since 1882.* New York: Hill and Wang, 2004.

Kraut, Alan M. *The Huddled Masses: The Immigrant in American Society, 1880–1921.* Arlington Heights, IL: Harlan Davidson, 1982.

National Park Service. Ellis Island. http://www.nps.gov/elis/.

Spickard, Paul. *Almost All Aliens: Immigration, Race, and Colonialism in American History and Identity.* New York: Routledge, 2007.

Taylor, Philip. *The Distant Magnet: European Emigration to the U.S.A.* New York: Harper & Row, 1971.

Annexation of Hawaii

The annexation of Hawaii in 1898 by the United States provided a strategic outpost in the Pacific Ocean for the projection of American influence. It was an important step in overseas expansion and is often identified as an early example of American imperialism.

For most of the nineteenth century, the Hawaiian Islands were a sovereign entity under a unified monarchy and recognized as such by major European powers and the United States. During the course of the century, a number of Westerners immigrated to the islands, beginning with American missionaries who succeeded in converting a substantial portion of the population to Protestant Christianity. The Hawaiian monarchy gradually conformed to Western legal norms, issuing a constitution and implementing a system of private property ownership that allowed Westerners to acquire legal title to land. In the 1870s, the Hawaiian government signed trade agreements with the United States, and sugar cultivation for export to the United States became a dominant part of the islands' economy. Large numbers of Asian immigrants also went to Hawaii to take part in the growing economy.

THE OVERTHROW OF LILIUOKALANI

Tensions escalated in the 1880s between the monarchy and a Westernizing group known as the Reform (or Missionary) Party, which believed that King Kalakaua (1836–1891) was fiscally irresponsible and a poor governor. In 1887, the Reform Party managed to impose a new constitution—called the Bayonet Constitution by its critics—on the king, greatly reducing his powers. European and American residents in Hawaii were granted suffrage, while most Asians lost it.

Renewed treaties with the United States permitted a permanent U.S. naval base at Pearl Harbor, which most native Hawaiians opposed. The death of King Kalakaua and the accession to the throne of his sister, Liliuokalani (1838–1917), in 1891 did not alleviate tensions. When the new queen attempted to draft a constitution that would restore the monarchy's power, the thirteen-member Committee of Safety—made up of Europeans and Americans—resolved to overthrow the monarchy and seek the annexation of Hawaii to the United States.

On January 16, 1893, at the request of the Committee of Safety (which alleged an imminent danger to U.S. citizens and their property), John L. Stevens (1820–1895), the Department of State's minister to Hawaii, summoned uniformed U.S. Marines and sailors to take up stations on Hawaiian soil. In effect, they assisted the Committee of Safety's 1,500 militiamen in their revolution against Queen Liliuokalani, who surrendered the following day. The new provisional government, led by Sanford B. Dole (1844–1926), was recognized as legitimate within days by all foreign powers with a diplomatic presence in Hawaii. The new government immediately petitioned Stevens for annexation, and in February outgoing U.S. President Benjamin Harrison (1833–1901) agreed to the proposal.

Before the U.S. Senate could ratify the proposed treaty, however, incoming President Grover Cleveland withdrew it from consideration pending an investigation of the role of U.S. government agents in the Hawaiian Revolution. James H. Blount (1837–1903), a former congressman from Georgia, conducted the investigation. In July, Blount reported that American diplomats and military officials had abused their authority and were responsible for Queen Liliuokalani's overthrow.

After her overthrow and unsuccessful attempts to prevent American annexation of Hawaii, Liliuokalani, shown here in a portrait dated March 8, 1915, lived privately in Honolulu until her death in 1917.

In his State of the Union address to Congress on December 4, 1893, President Grover Cleveland summarized the results of Blount's investigation and condemned the alleged American abetment of the Hawaiian Revolution:

"After a thorough and exhaustive examination Mr. Blount submitted to me his report, showing beyond all question that the constitutional Government of Hawaii had been subverted with the active aid of our representative to that Government and through the intimidation caused by the presence of an armed naval force."

President Cleveland recalled Stevens and turned the matter over to Congress, which concluded after further investigation, as detailed in the Morgan Report of February 1894, that Stevens and the American military were not to blame for the revolution. In the aftermath of the congressional investigation, Cleveland abandoned efforts to reinstate Liliuokalani, but also refused to follow through on the annexation of Hawaii.

ANNEXATION

Rebuffed by Cleveland, Hawaii's provisional government made plans for operation as an independent entity, declaring the Republic of Hawaii on July 4, 1894. The new republic's constitution had a standing clause providing for Hawaii's annexation by the United States, and Dole's government continued to lobby officials in Washington, D.C., to that end. From the Hawaiian perspective, a primary rationale for annexation was economic. As part of the United States, Hawaiian sugar exports—the backbone of the islands' economy—would not be subject to U.S. tariffs. Nevertheless, many native Hawaiians and Asian immigrants opposed annexation. Their resistance to the new government led to an attempted counterrevolution in 1895, but the uprising failed and Liliuokalani was imprisoned.

In 1897, William McKinley (1843–1901) succeeded Grover Cleveland as U.S. president and brought to the White House a more expansionist vision than his predecessor. The most formidable obstacle to Hawaiian annexation, Cleveland himself, had thus been removed. In July 1898, Congress passed and McKinley signed the Newlands Resolution, which provided for the annexation of Hawaii. The following month, the Dole government formally transferred sovereignty to the United States. On February 22, 1900, the islands officially became Hawaii Territory, with Dole as governor.

PLATFORM OF INFLUENCE

Historians have pointed to U.S. involvement in Hawaii as the first overt example of U.S. overseas imperialism, soon to be followed by the Spanish-American War (1898) and expansion in Latin America and the Pacific Ocean. The annexation of Hawaii guaranteed the continued presence of an American naval base in the South Pacific as a platform from which the United States could project its influence farther toward Asia. In addition, Pacific expansion would provide incentives for other important American actions in the early twentieth century, such as the construction of the Panama Canal.

Although a government commission in the early 1980s reaffirmed that the United States was not at fault during the events of the 1890s, Congress in 1993 passed a bill, later signed by President Bill Clinton (1946–), that formally apologized to the people of Hawaii for any violations of their sovereignty.

Jason E. Jewell

GUIDED READING

Coffman, Tom. *Nation Within: The Story of America's Annexation of the Nation of Hawaii.* Kane'ohe, HI: Epicenter, 1998.

Dole, Sanford B. *Memoirs of the Hawaiian Revolution.* Honolulu, HI: Advertiser Publishing, 1936.

Kinzer, Stephen. *Overthrow: America's Century of Regime Change from Hawaii to Iraq.* New York: Times Books/Henry Holt, 2006.

Liliuokalani, Queen of Hawaii. *Hawaii's Story by Hawaii's Queen.* Rutland, VT: C.E. Tuttle, 1964.

THE SPANISH-AMERICAN WAR (1898)

The Spanish-American War confirmed the emergence of the United States as a world power and resulted in a dramatic expansion of the nation's overseas possessions.

While the countries of Europe were engaged in an imperial rivalry to acquire overseas colonies in Asia and Africa, the United States had expanded westward across North America. By the 1890s, with most of the country settled, enthusiasm for expansion elsewhere swelled. Some argued for continued expansion to gain access to new markets and raw materials, which would allow the United States to export more products to areas that restricted imported goods, while eliminating taxes on the export of raw materials.

Others contended that the United States needed additional territories for national security reasons. They wanted areas such as Hawaii, the Philippines, and the Caribbean to serve as U.S. naval bases and refueling stations.

A third group of expansionists believed that the United States had a duty to rule areas populated by other races. This idea was known as Social Darwinism, a belief that some races were more advanced than others. Social Darwinism incorporated the noted scientist Charles Darwin's ideas on evolution into a theory that certain races had evolved or advanced more quickly than others.

THE CUBAN STRUGGLE

Once the largest colonial power in the Americas, by the late 1800s Spain held only Cuba and Puerto Rico as colonies. The United States, Great Britain, and France supported independence for the remaining Spanish colonies in order to open trade and gain influence in Cuba in Puerto Rico.

In 1895, Cubans launched an insurrection to gain independence from Spain. Some 200,000 Cubans were killed, mainly civilians who died from disease and starvation when they were forced into relocation camps. Spain remained committed to retaining the colony because of the island's rich sugarcane plantations, which provided a significant source of income for the Spanish government in Madrid.

In the United States, the revolutionary movement had broad support among many Americans who saw parallels between the Cuban struggle and the American Revolution. Other Americans supported Cuban independence because they wanted access to economic markets on the island that were restricted by the Spanish government through tariffs, customs duties, and limitations on foreign ownership of land. There were also large Cuban immigrant populations in New York, Tampa, and Key West that endorsed independence for the island.

YELLOW JOURNALISM

While the Cuban conflict simmered, competition among rival newspapers in the United States led to the rise of what became known as yellow journalism. Against the backdrop of the Cuban insurrection, two titans of the newspaper industry, William Randolph Hearst and Joseph

Alfred Thayer Mahan was a military scholar and one of the leading U.S. proponents of a strong navy and control of the seas. He influenced generations of military and political leaders, including Theodore Roosevelt.

Relations between the United States and Great Britain were strained on the eve of the Spanish-American War. In 1895, the two countries almost went to war over a boundary dispute in Venezuela, which was soon resolved. As tensions with Spain escalated in 1896, the British worked with U.S. diplomats to isolate Spain from gaining European supporters. The British then worked with the United States during the Spanish-American War. In exchange, the United States offered Great Britain diplomatic support and cooperation during future conflicts. This pattern of cooperation laid the foundation for what became known as the special relationship between the two countries that started with World War I and continues to the present day.

Pulitzer, became locked in a fierce competition for readers.

In February 1898, Pulitzer's *New York Journal* published a letter from the Spanish ambassador to the United States, Enrique Dupuy de Lôme, in which the ambassador criticized Republican President William McKinley as weak and pandering to the public. Americans were outraged, and the ambassador was forced to resign. Less than a week later, on February 15, a battle-

ship, the USS *Maine*, exploded in the harbor in Havana, Cuba. The ship had been dispatched as a sign of U.S. strength, but the explosion sank the vessel and killed 260 American sailors.

Played out in the newspapers, blame for the *Maine* rested squarely on Spain. Public pressure mounted on the McKinley administration, and the United States issued an ultimatum in March calling for Spain to withdraw from Cuba or face war. The Spanish government offered

WILLIAM RANDOLPH HEARST (1863–1951)

William Randolph Hearst dramatically changed the way newspapers reported events. His wealthy father acquired *The San Francisco Examiner*, and Hearst took over the paper in 1887. The young newspaperman bought a number of other papers and soon became embroiled in competitive bid for readers. Hearst began to publish ever more sensational headlines and stories. He took advantage of advances in publishing technology, including the invention of the linotype in Great Britain in 1896, to publish papers more quickly and at a lower cost. In 1898, Hearst used his newspapers to highlight real and imagined atrocities and repression in Cuba, and rallied public opinion in favor of war against Spain. The success of Hearst's journalistic style led newspapers in the United States, France, and Great Britain to emulate yellow journalism to increase sales. Hearst's fame and success led to a significant increase in the number of writers who became war correspondents, including the future British Prime Minister Winston Churchill.

After the USS *Maine* was raised following its sinking in Havana harbor, the U.S. Navy concluded that an internal explosion destroyed the *Maine*, not a Spanish attack.

a Spanish force in Manila Bay. The war began when the U.S. commander Commodore George Dewey uttered the phrase, "You may fire when you are ready, Gridley" to Charles Gridley, the captain of his flagship.

The naval victory was followed by a declaration of independence by Philippine rebels who had fought an unsuccessful revolution in 1896, and a land campaign in which U.S. troops and Philippine rebels together defeated Spanish forces, but it wasn't until after the war ended that Spain accepted the independence of the islands.

Annexing U.S. Conquests

In June, U.S. forces captured the Spanish-held island of Guam without firing a shot. There were only 55 Spanish soldiers on the island, and they were unaware that they were even at war. The remote island, 1,500 miles (2,400 kilometers) east of the Philippines and 3,000 miles (4,800 kilometers) west of Hawaii, has remained American territory ever since, and is used as a refueling station for the U.S. navy to the present day.

The Philippines were seen as a gateway to the lucrative markets of China. Several nations, including Germany and Japan, dispatched naval forces to the Philippines in an effort to gain influence over the newly independent islands. News of foreign forces in Manila Bay concerned the McKinley administration, which came under pressure from a coalition of business leaders and imperialists to annex the Philippines in order to keep other countries out.

The administration's decision in 1899 to go forward with annexation stirred anti-imperialist sentiment in the United States. Some anti-imperialists were philosophically opposed to the acquisition of territory by force, while others feared products from these areas would cost American jobs because goods and resources could be produced for lower costs than in the United States.

concessions, but they were too late. McKinley and his advisors realized that public sentiment for war was so strong that the Republicans risked electoral defeat in the upcoming congressional elections if they did not act. On April 11, 1898, the president asked Congress for a declaration of war.

While there was general support for war, many Americans opposed the territorial expansion of the United States. Consequently, although Congress voted 311 to 6 in the House of Representatives and 42 to 35 in the Senate in favor of war on April 20, 1898, it included the Teller Amendment, named after Colorado Senator Henry Moore Teller. The Teller Amendment forbade the United States from making Cuba a colony.

WAR WITH SPAIN

Although the Spanish-American War centered on Cuba, early fighting actually took place halfway across the world in the Pacific Ocean near another Spanish colony—the Philippines. On May 1, 1898, a U.S. naval squadron defeated

Land Action in Cuba

In the Caribbean, the United States initiated a naval blockade around the Spanish-held colonies of Cuba and Puerto Rico. The first U.S. troops landed in Cuba on June 10, 1898. Cuban rebels and U.S. forces won a quick series of victories, culminating with the capture of Santiago on July 17. The following day, the Spanish government asked the United States for a truce and negotiated a peace settlement. France sponsored the initial negotiations since it was regarded by both the United States and Spain as a neutral party in the conflict.

During the negotiations, Whitelaw Reid of the United States claimed that the U.S. goal was "for American energy to build up such a commercial marine on the Pacific Coast as should ultimately convert the Pacific Ocean into an American lake, making it far more our own than the Atlantic Ocean is now Great Britain's.

On July 25, a U.S. force captured Puerto Rico. On August 12, Spain and the United States signed a formal peace protocol in Washington, D.C., which ended hostilities. The Treaty of Paris ended the war. It was signed in Paris, France, on December 10, 1898. The U.S. Senate ratified the Treaty of Paris by a vote of 52 to 27 on February 6, 1899.

AFTERMATH AND CONSEQUENCES

The Spanish-American War cost the United States approximately $250 million. In total, 3,289 U.S. soldiers and sailors died in the war, of

THE DEBATE OVER ANNEXING THE PHILIPPINES

In January 1900, Republican Senator Alfred Beveridge of Indiana delivered a speech before Congress. In it, he summarized the strategic reasons for annexation at the time:

"The Philippines give us a base at the door of all the East."

Many Americans, however, were uncomfortable with the idea of the United States acquiring new territory as a result of war with Spain. Democratic Presidential candidate William Jennings Bryan argued against annexation. During his 1900 campaign speech, he said:

"We do not want the Filipinos for citizens. They cannot, without danger to us, share in the government of our nation and moreover, we cannot afford to add another race question to the race questions which we already have."

which 432 died in combat and the remainder died from tropical diseases such as malaria and yellow fever.

Under the terms of the Treaty of Paris, the United States gained possession of Guam, the Philippines and Puerto Rico, in exchange for a payment of $20 million to the Spanish government in Madrid. The people of the Philippines

An expeditionary force of 17,000 troops was dispatched from Tampa, Florida, to invade Cuba. The U.S. forces included a regiment of volunteer cavalry, the "Rough Riders," led by future president and ardent expansionist, Theodore Roosevelt

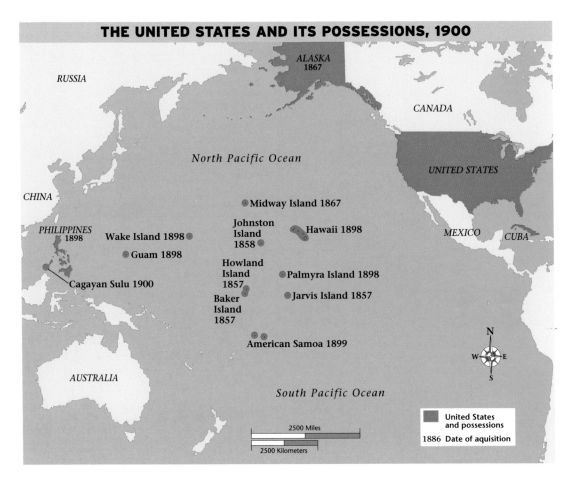

THE UNITED STATES AND ITS POSSESSIONS, 1900

did not respond favorably to U.S. annexation, and a bloody independence insurgency there lasted until 1902.

Congress authorized the annexation of the Hawaiian Islands in June 1898, and the United States continued to acquire territory dotted around the Pacific Ocean, including Wake Island in January 1899.

In accordance with the Teller Amendment, Cuba was granted independence, yet it remained under U.S. military control until 1902. Congress then enacted the Platt Amendment, which gave the United States the right to maintain a military base at Guantanamo Bay, as well as the authority to intervene to maintain order or financial stability—a clause that would later be used to justify successive American military interventions in Cuba.

The Spanish-American War ushered in an era of U.S. interventionism in Latin America, the Caribbean, China, and Africa. The United States continued its military rise and, as president, Theodore Roosevelt dispatched a fleet of 16 ships (known as the Great White Fleet) around the world to demonstrate American power.

Roosevelt declared in his 1902 address to Congress that "a good navy is not a provocation to war. It is the surest guaranty of peace." With its increased military capabilities, the country became more assertive in expanding its role in the Western Hemisphere and countering European efforts to gain influence in the region.

Tom Lansford

GUIDED READING

Bradford, James, ed. *Crucible of Empire: The Spanish-American War and Its Aftermath*. Annapolis, MD: Naval Institute, 1996.

Crucible of Empire. The Spanish-American War. http://www.pbs.org/crucible/.

Offner, John L. *An Unwanted War: The Diplomacy of the United States and Spain Over Cuba, 1895–1898*. Chapel Hill: University of North Carolina Press, 1992.

Scott, Edward van Zile. 1996. *The Unwept: Black Soldiers and the Spanish-American War*. Montgomery, AL: Black Belt, 1996.

THE OPEN DOOR POLICY AND BOXER REBELLION

The phrase "Open Door policy" refers to the United States' advocacy of free trade in China during the early twentieth century. Attempts to create a free-trade regime among the great powers with Chinese interests were hampered by the Boxer Rebellion, in which Chinese subjects attacked foreign legations in Beijing and provoked an international armed response.

In the eighteenth and nineteenth centuries, various European states placed a high value on trade with China, a producer of silk, porcelain, and tea, all of which were in strong demand in Europe. China's Qing Dynasty, however, strictly limited trade with the West to the port of Canton (Guangzhou) and refused to deal with foreign governments unless they acknowledged tributary status to the Chinese emperor. Moreover, Chinese merchants demonstrated little appetite for Western goods. In the early nineteenth century, Great Britain found a solution to the latter problem in the export to China of opium from British-controlled India.

MOST FAVORED NATIONS

Chinese demand for opium soared by the 1830s, angering the Qing authorities, whose attempts to stop the opium trade by seizing British ships and merchandise led to the First Opium War (1839–1842). With British victory in that conflict, the resulting Treaty of Nanjing (1842) required that China, among other things, open more ports to foreign trade and grant Great Britain most-favored-nation trade status.

Britain and France clashed with China in the Second Opium War (1856–1858), which resulted in another Chinese defeat and further concessions in the Treaty of Tientsin (1858). Even more Chinese ports were opened to foreign trade, Europeans were allowed to travel into China's interior (including the capital city, Beijing, where foreign legations were now established for the first time), and Christian missionaries were permitted to evangelize the Chinese population.

In the second half of the nineteenth century, other European powers such as France, Russia, and Germany managed to negotiate most-

favored-nation trade status with the Qing Dynasty, thereby gaining the same trading privileges enjoyed by Great Britain. The result was a process whereby each European nation carved out an economic—and indirectly political—sphere of influence for itself in Chinese territory, establishing commercial networks that reached to the nation's interior. Even Japan, which was rapidly modernizing in the late nineteenth century, joined the scramble for economic influence in China, defeating the latter in the Sino-Japanese War (1894–1895) and creating its own spheres of influence in Formosa (modern Taiwan) and Port Arthur, a port town in southern Manchuria that Japan seized after the war. By 1900, despite nominal unity and continued Qing governance, China had fallen largely under the control of foreign imperialistic powers.

During the First Opium War, a relatively small portion of the British fleet easily defeated China's navy, which was unsophisticated by Western standards.

OPEN DOOR POLICY

The United States—having only begun expansion in the Pacific region in the late 1890s with the annexation of Hawaii and conquest of the Philippines in the Spanish-American War—also sought to benefit from Chinese markets. President William McKinley, believing China was a logical market for growing American exports, attempted to penetrate the Asian giant's economy with a consortium of U.S. cotton, railroad, and mining interests—calling itself the American Asiatic Association. This organization, originally called the Committee on American Interests in China, had formed in early 1898 to seek cooperation with European powers in Chinese markets.

On September 6, 1899, U.S. Secretary of State John Hay (1838–1905) sent a series of notes to the governments of Great Britain, Germany, and Russia, with similar memoranda later communicated to France, Italy, and Japan. In these messages, Hay called for an Open Door policy in China to replace the spheres-of-influence system that was currently in place.

The responses to Hays's overtures were cautious, with most of the recipients indicating that they would agree to the proposal only if all the other interested powers did so as well. Hay interpreted these equivocations as an endorsement of his policy and made public announcements to that effect. Before any real changes could take place, however, the Open Door idea suffered a major setback in the form of the Boxer Rebellion.

A REBELLION TO DRIVE OUT FOREIGNERS

The Society of Right and Harmonious Fists—called "Boxers" by Westerners because of its use of martial arts—was a secret, anti-Western society in China that received surreptitious support from the Qing Dynasty. In 1898, Boxers began attacks on Chinese Christians in the northern part of the country. These attacks increased in scale and intensity over the following two years, and by early 1900 thousands of Chinese Christians had been killed, along with some foreign missionaries. In June 1900, the rebellion escalated when tens of thousands of Boxers entered Beijing and attacked foreign legations, killing 231 foreigners. The remainder were evacuated to a fortified compound, which remained under siege for weeks.

Western response to the Boxer Rebellion was swift. In August, a coalition of 54,000 troops from eight nations, including the United States (which contributed more than 3,000 soldiers), occupied Beijing after inflicting heavy damage

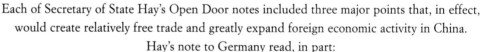

HAY'S FIRST OPEN DOOR NOTE TO GERMANY (1899)

Each of Secretary of State Hay's Open Door notes included three major points that, in effect, would create relatively free trade and greatly expand foreign economic activity in China.

Hay's note to Germany read, in part:

"[T]he Government of the United States would be pleased to see His German Majesty's Government give formal assurances, and lend its cooperation in securing like assurances from the other interested powers, that each, within its respective sphere of whatever influence—

First. Will in no way interfere with any treaty port or any vested interest within any so-called 'sphere of influence' or leased territory it may have in China.

Second. That the Chinese treaty tariff of the time being shall apply to all merchandise landed or shipped to all such ports as are within said 'sphere of influence' (unless they be 'free ports'), no matter to what nationality it may belong, and that duties so leviable shall be collected by the Chinese Government.

Third. That it will levy no higher harbor dues on vessels of another nationality frequenting any port in such 'sphere' than shall be levied on vessels of its own nationality, and no higher railroad charges over lines built, controlled, or operated within its 'sphere' on merchandise belonging to citizens or subjects of other nationalities transported through such 'sphere' than shall be levied on similar merchandise belonging to its own nationals transported over equal distances."

As part of their rebellion against the West, the Boxers bombed the railway station in Tientsin, China.

on the Boxers. The Qing government was forced to pay a large indemnity to the eight nations as punishment for its support of the Boxers. The United States eventually returned almost half of its share of the fine to create a trust fund used to support Chinese students in both China and the United States.

Hay, now receiving no substantive cooperation on trade from the other Western powers, unilaterally issued a second round of Open Door notes to U.S. envoys on July 3, 1900. The message reaffirmed U.S. commitment to an Open Door policy that would be beneficial to all parties involved, including China. In fact, Hay was hoping to persuade China to accept U.S. mediation in its negotiations with other powers and to align Chinese and American economic interests. In succeeding years, while other powers occasionally agreed in principle, the Open Door policy was never fully implemented. It effectively died in the 1930s, when Japan established the puppet state of Manchukuo in Chinese Manchuria.

Jason E. Jewell

GUIDED READING

Cohen, Paul A. *History in Three Keys: The Boxers as Event, Experience, and Myth.* New York: Columbia University Press, 1997.

Esherick, Joseph W. *The Origins of the Boxer Uprising.* Berkeley: University of California Press, 1987.

McKee, Delber L. *Chinese Exclusion Versus the Open Door Policy, 1900–1906: Clashes over China Policy in the Roosevelt Era.* Detroit, MI: Wayne State University Press, 1977.

Preston, Diana. *The Boxer Rebellion: The Dramatic Story of China's War on Foreigners that Shook the World in the Summer of 1900.* New York: Walker, 2000.

THE RUSSO-JAPANESE WAR AND PORTSMOUTH CONFERENCE

The Russo-Japanese War (1904–1905) grew out of imperialist designs harbored by both nations on Manchuria and Korea. The Portsmouth Conference held at the end of the war produced a peace settlement brokered by the United States that established Japan as a rising world power and helped set the stage for the Russian Revolution of 1917. The Portsmouth Treaty, while ending the war, ultimately damaged the relationship between the United States and Japan.

Japan's imperialist notions grew from the Meiji Restoration of 1868, which resulted in a new regime that began a program of rapid Westernization. By coming out of isolation, Japan hoped to compete on the world stage with Western powers, in part by expanding its commercial networks and influence in East Asia.

Russia also sought to expand its influence in the East, bringing the Russians into direct conflict with Japanese interests. As Japan attempted to gain control of Korea, the Russians were able to force the Chinese into a treaty that granted them control of Port Arthur, a key Pacific port city on the Liaodong Peninsula in southern Manchuria that had been occupied by Japan. The Russians took immediate steps to consolidate their power in the region and began building a railroad into Manchuria. In response, Japan sought an agreement with Russia to carve out spheres of influence in the area, but the Russians were not receptive. Concerned over the Russian presence in Manchuria, and certain that the Russians would continue to expand their influence if given the opportunity, Japan chose to go to war.

Japanese troops dug in near the town of Tieling just before the Battle of Mukden, the last major land battle of the Russo-Japanese War.

THE RUSSO-JAPANESE WAR

The fighting began on February 8, 1904, when Japan launched a surprise attack on the Russian navy in Port Arthur. The Russians completely underestimated the Japanese military and will to fight. During the next few months, Japan successfully invaded Korea and landed a significant force on China's Liaodong Peninsula. The Japanese won victories at Fuhsien and Liaoyang, and in January 1905 the Russians surrendered Port Arthur. An exceedingly bloody Japanese victory took place at Mukden in March, during which more than 90,000 Russians were killed and wounded before withdrawing; the Japanese suffered more than 75,000 casualties. Then in May, Japanese forces crushed the Russian navy at the Battle of Tsushima. But Russia refused to surrender, and Japan began having financial difficulties caused by the war. Both sides wanted to end the fighting, and, at the request of Japan, U.S. President Theodore Roosevelt (1858–1909) stepped in to mediate.

Representatives from Russia and Japan gathered around a conference table in Portsmouth, New Hampshire, to begin negotiations to end the Russo-Japanese War. Theodore Roosevelt would win the 1906 Nobel Peace prize for his role in mediating the conflict.

THE PORTSMOUTH CONFERENCE

The Peace Conference that ended the Russo-Japanese War was held from August 9 through September 5, 1905, in Portsmouth, New Hampshire. After a month of negotiations led by President Roosevelt, the warring parties signed the Treaty of Portsmouth. Under the terms of the accord, Japan and Russia both agreed to withdraw from Manchuria; Japan received the rights to Port Arthur through a lease agreement as well as other territory in the Pacific. In the process, President Roosevelt also extracted from the Japanese a reluctant agreement to cease territorial expansion in the Pacific.

The final treaty was a triumph for President Roosevelt, who received the 1906 Nobel Peace Prize for his efforts. But the end of the Russo-Japanese War had far-reaching repercussions. In Russia, the defeat was a blow to the czar's regime that destabilized the government and set the country on a path toward revolution.

In Japan, the military victory marked the nation's emergence as a great power on the world stage. The Treaty of Portsmouth was not well received by the Japanese public, which saw the American president as an opportunist and resented his demand that Japan cease its expansion in the Pacific. After the treaty signing, the relationship between the United States and Japan began to deteriorate.

Ben Wynne

MAKING PEACE

In presenting the 1906 Nobel Peace Prize to Theodore Roosevelt, the official spokesman of the Nobel Committee declared:

"The United States of America was among the first to infuse the ideal of peace into practical politics. Peace and arbitration treaties have now been concluded between the United States and the governments of several countries. But what has especially directed the attention of the friends of peace and of the whole civilized world to the United States is President Roosevelt's happy role in bringing to an end the bloody war recently waged between two of the world's great powers, Japan and Russia."

GUIDED READING

Gould, Lewis L. *The Presidency of Theodore Roosevelt*. Lawrence: University Press of Kansas, 1991.

Jukes, Geoffrey. *The Russo-Japanese War 1904–1905*. Oxford, UK: Osprey, 2002.

The Russo-Japanese War Research Society. http://www.russojapanesewar.com.

Warner, Denis Ashton, and Peggy Warner. *The Tide at Sunrise: A History of the Russo-Japanese War, 1904–1905*. Portland, OR: Frank Cass, 2002.

THE PANAMA CANAL

Completion of the 51-mile (82-kilometer) Panama Canal during the early twentieth century linked the waters of the Atlantic and Pacific oceans, demonstrated the U.S. policy of domination in Central America, and provided a lasting legacy for the presidential administration of Theodore Roosevelt.

The strategic importance of the Isthmus of Panama, a small strip of land that connects North America and South America, was apparent to the first Spanish explorers who entered the region during the early sixteenth century. Beginning in 1513, when Vasco Núñez de Balboa (1475–1519) became the first European to travel west across the isthmus to the Pacific Ocean, the Spanish built roads and attempted to move ships, supplies, and plunder stolen from local native tribes.

Talk of building a canal that would provide a shorter water route from the Atlantic to the Pacific began during the 1530s, but the massive scope of such a project and the technological limitations of the period put any real prospects centuries into the future. The Spanish did conduct surveys to determine the best route for a

canal in Central America, considering a channel through Nicaragua—or even the southern portion of Mexico—as well. Aside from periodic improvements to local roads, however, there was little improvement in transportation across the Isthmus of Panama for almost three centuries.

THE MODERN ERA

During the nineteenth century, as the world began to industrialize and global commerce increased, the need for improved transportation across Central America became obvious to industrialists, entrepreneurs, and government officials around the world. In the United States, interest in getting from the Atlantic to the Pacific intensified after the discovery of gold in California in 1848 and the need to transport vast numbers of people and products to the fast-

During the 1850s, before building the canal, the United States sponsored construction of a rail line across the Isthmus of Panama. It soon became one of the most heavily used freight railways in the world.

growing state. By then, the Isthmus of Panama was part of Colombia, which had broken away from Spain earlier in the century. Between 1850 and 1855, private interests primarily from the United States constructed the Panama Railway across the isthmus. The rail line soon became one of the most heavily traveled freight railways in the world, and it set the stage for the building of the canal.

FRENCH ATTEMPTS

Interest in the construction of a waterway across Panama peaked during the 1870s, following the successful completion of the Suez Canal in Egypt. In 1879, Ferdinand Marie de Lesseps (1805–1894), who had constructed the Suez Canal, organized a French company, Compagnie Univeselle du Canal Interoceanique, to begin work in Panama. De Lesseps estimated that construction would take 12 years to complete, at a cost of approximately $130 million. The French broke ground in January 1882 but quickly encountered problems. De Lesseps and his engineers had underestimated the severity of the Panamanian rainy season, and the local rainforests became almost impenetrable. Workers, waist deep in mud and facing miles of jungle swamp, could find no refuge from the swarms of mosquitoes that bred in the region. Malaria and other insect-borne diseases reached epidemic proportions. Within a few years, it was evident that the project was a disaster.

By 1889, when the Compagnie Univeselle du Canal Interoceanique went bankrupt, 11 miles (18 kilometers) of the canal had been dug at a price of millions of dollars and an estimated 21,000 lives. French investors in the enterprise lost their money; some charged fraud or outright theft. During the 1890s, the Compagnie Universelle du Canal Interoceanique reorganized and made a second attempt to complete the canal, but once again they were forced to abandon the project.

PANAMANIAN INDEPENDENCE AND U.S. OCCUPATION

Upon becoming president of the United States in 1901, Theodore Roosevelt took steps to ensure U.S. completion and control of the canal across Panama. Determined to expand the influence of the United States around the globe, Roosevelt believed that the United States had

the sole right to intervene in Latin America and that a canal through Central America was of utmost strategic importance. Some American politicians favored a canal through Nicaragua, but President Roosevelt wanted the United States to finish the job that the French had started in Panama.

Because Panama was still a Colombian province, the United States opened negotiations with the Colombian government for the rights to complete the canal. President Roosevelt sent Secretary of State John Hay to talk with the Colombians, but discussions quickly turned contentious. Under the Hay-Herran Treaty, signed in January 1903, the United States agreed to pay Colombia $10 million and an annual fee for the rights to build and maintain the canal. The Colombian Senate refused to ratify the agreement, however, and government negotiators raised their demand to an upfront payment of at least $20 million. Furious, President Roosevelt made plans to bypass the Colombian government altogether.

❝ ROOSEVELT TAKES CHARGE ❞

Theodore Roosevelt considered the Panama Canal one of the greatest achievements of his administration. During a speech at the University of California in 1911, he declared:
"There are plenty of other things I started merely because the time had come that whoever was in power would have started them. But the Panama Canal would not have started if I had not taken hold of it, because if I had followed the traditional or conservative method I should have submitted an admirable state paper to Congress ... and the beginning of work on the canal would be fifty years in the future. ... Accordingly I took the isthmus, started the canal and then left Congress not to debate the canal, but to debate me."

The Roosevelt administration responded to Colombia's demands by promoting a revolution in Panama and promising U.S. assistance. In 1903, the Panamanians mounted a nationalist uprising and declared independence from Colombia, and the United States sent naval forces to the area to protect the fledgling nation

Thousands of workers, most of whom came from Central America and the Caribbean, braved the heat, humidity, and exposure to various tropical diseases to construct the canal.

from the Colombians. The United States was the first nation to recognize Panama's independence and immediately entered into negotiations for the right to build the canal. Grateful for their new status as an independent nation, the Panamanians in 1904 accepted the $10 million offer originally made to Colombia.

The United States and Panama signed the Hay-Bunau Varilla Treaty (1904), giving the Americans the rights in perpetuity to a 10-mile (16-kilometer) strip of land (called the Canal Zone) across the isthmus, through which the canal would be completed. The United States took full control of the area, raised the American flag, and restricted the Panamanians from entering. The Canal Zone had its own governor and its own political and economic infrastructure. Within its boundaries, the United States would build military bases as well as the canal.

In 1904, the United States resumed construction of the Panama Canal, using state-of-the-art equipment that had not been available to the French. Two years later, President Roosevelt visited the Canal Zone to observe the progress of the project, which he considered one of his greatest achievements as president. The Panama Canal was completed in 1914 at an estimated cost of more than $350 million. During the period of construction, approximately 350 American workers died, along with more than 5,600 laborers from various parts of Central America and

THOMSON-URRUTIA TREATY (1921)

The relationship between the United States and Colombia soured as a result of President Roosevelt's role in helping Panama gain independence in 1904. During the tenure of President Woodrow Wilson, however, the United States began efforts to establish better relations with the Colombians. In 1914, President Wilson sent Thaddeus A. Thomson (1853–1927), a lawyer and diplomat, to Bogotá, Colombia's capital, to negotiate a treaty with the Colombians that included restitution for the loss of Panama. The result was the Thomson-Urrutia Treaty, under which the United States agreed to pay Colombia $25 million for the loss. The Colombians signed the accord, but Republicans in the U.S. Senate, including a number of Roosevelt's old political allies, mustered enough votes to defeat the treaty. Seven years later, at the behest of American businessmen interested in Colombian oil reserves, the treaty was revived and ratified in another attempt to repair relations between the two countries.

the Caribbean. The first ship passed through the Panama Canal on August 15, 1914, albeit with little fanfare because of the onset of World War I in Europe.

The United States controlled the canal and the Canal Zone for more than 80 years. Following World War II (1939–1945), administration of the region began causing friction between the United States and Panama. Many Panamanians resented the American presence in their homeland and staged periodic protests. At first, the United States increased its military presence in the region, but this led to more unrest. Finally in 1977, U.S. President Jimmy Carter (1924–) signed treaties with the Panamanian regime that began the process of relinquishing U.S. control of the canal. Panama officially took control of the waterway at the end of 1999.

Ben Wynne

Led by a tugboat, a ship makes its way through the newly opened Panama Canal during the early twentieth century.

GUIDED READING

Lafeber, Walter. *Panama Canal: The Crisis in Historical Perspective.* New York: Oxford University Press, 1989.

McCullough, David G. *The Path Between the Seas: The Creation of the Panama Canal, 1870–1914.* New York: Simon & Schuster, 1977.

The Panama Canal Authority. http://www.pancanal.com.

Parker, Matthew. *Panama Fever: The Epic Story of One of the Greatest Human Achievements of All Time—the Building of the Panama Canal.* New York: Doubleday, 2007.

American Interventions in Mexico and the Caribbean

As European power faded in the Western Hemisphere during the nineteenth century, the United States quickly became the regional power and exerted its dominance over Mexico and the Caribbean.

The Caribbean region has had a long history of foreign interference and domination, and Europe's great powers were in constant competition over its vast resources to facilitate their imperial ambitions. Spain, to begin with, enjoyed a monopoly in the region for nearly two centuries. By the end of the seventeenth century, almost all its possessions in the region had been conquered by European rivals, whom—it has been argued—may have had to attack Spain in the Americas in order to defeat it in Europe.

The mantle of domination in the Caribbean quickly passed from Spain to the United States—close in proximity to the region and now a powerful country—as the latter had implemented an exclusivist policy toward the entire region and regarded it as being under their sole influence.

RISE OF U.S. INTERVENTIONISM

The Monroe Doctrine (1823) had a two-fold strategy—to keep the European powers out of the Caribbean while keeping the United States in. Although the British, French, Dutch, and Danes managed to hold on to their possessions, U.S. success in the Spanish-American War of

President James Monroe (*standing*) and key cabinet officials discussed the proposal to extend the American sphere of influence over the Western Hemisphere, known as the Monroe Doctrine (1823).

THE ROOSEVELT COROLLARY

The Roosevelt Corollary was an amendment to the Monroe Doctrine made in 1904 by President Theodore Roosevelt, who argued that the United States was justified in intervening in Caribbean nations if they were unable to pay their foreign debts. In his Annual Message to Congress in December 1904, Roosevelt said:

"All that this country desires is to see the neighboring countries stable, orderly, and prosperous. Any country whose people conduct themselves well can count upon our hearty friendship. If a nation shows that it knows how to act with reasonable efficiency and decency in social and political matters, if it keeps order and pays its obligations, it need fear no interference from the United States. Chronic wrongdoing, or an impotence which results in a general loosening of the ties of civilized society, may in America, as elsewhere, ultimately require intervention by some civilized nation, and in the Western Hemisphere the adherence of the United States to the Monroe Doctrine may force the United States, however reluctantly, in flagrant cases of such wrongdoing or impotence, to the exercise of an international police power."

1898 gave the government in Washington additional confidence in extending U.S. spheres of influence in the Western Hemisphere.

The opening of the Panama Canal in 1914 added another layer of strategic importance to the region, as U.S. policy makers realized that American control of the key shipping route would be not only advantageous, but also imperative. American policy makers at the time realized that the Caribbean would play a central role in U.S. politics for some time.

The Roosevelt Corollary

The United States intervened numerous times in the Caribbean during the first three decades of the twentieth century, but intervention was typically disguised as some form of benign action rather than as a form of imperialism. The interventions were typically aimed at providing political stability, protecting U.S strategic interests, making the area safe for business, and deterring European interests in the region.

The Roosevelt Corollary was an extension of the Monroe Doctrine in 1904 and a further attempt by the United States to maintain total control in Central America. In it, President Theodore Roosevelt declared that the United States would adopt a "protectorate policy" in the region. The Roosevelt Corollary remained in effect until the early 1930s, providing the rationale for numerous American regional

MAIN U.S. MILITARY INTERVENTIONS

Cuba (1906–1910, 1961)

Panama (1908, 1925)

Guatemala (1954)

Honduras (1907)

Nicaragua (1909–1911, 1912–1925 and 1926–1933)

Haiti (1915–1934)

Mexico (1916)

Dominican Republic (1916–1924)

interventions—especially in the Dominican Republic, Haiti, Nicaragua, and Mexico.

Dollar Diplomacy

When small Caribbean and Central American states could not make international debt payments, the United States often stepped in to help stabilize their economies. Many of these small nations were in debt to European powers, and President William Howard Taft's (1857–1930) use of "dollar diplomacy" was another form of intervention—non-military—in the region. Exerting influence through economic dominance was highly effective, although the use of dollar diplomacy ended with the Taft administration in 1913 because the incoming president, Woodrow Wilson, repudiated the policy.

The Banana Wars

U.S. military interventions known as the Banana Wars began with the 1898 Spanish-American War and continued until the Good Neighbor policy of 1934. Economic concerns were often the reason behind U.S. involvement in Latin America. The Banana Wars exemplified the influence of American corporate conglomerates, such as the United Fruit Company, in the region. The sole purpose of many of the armed campaigns was to protect U.S. commercial interests. Indeed some countries became known as banana republics because of the influence wielded by U.S. corporations in their national governments.

INTERVENTION IN MEXICO

As in the Caribbean, American interest in Mexico was largely economic—although a number of U.S. presidents, beginning with Abraham Lincoln (1809–1865) during the Civil War, wished to see Mexico achieve a stable and durable democratic system. At the beginning of the twentieth century, heavy investments in Mexico by American industry further increased interest in political and economic affairs south of the border.

While President Taft attempted to influence Mexico through economic means, President Wilson became embroiled in more forceful interventions. A relatively minor incident known as the Tampico Affair began on April 9, 1914, when Mexican forces loyal to General Adolfo de la Huerta (1854–1916) arrested nine U.S. soldiers for allegedly entering a prohibited zone in Tampico, an important port on Mexico's east coast 200 miles (320 kilometers) north of Veracruz. Diplomatic relations between the two countries broke down and resulted in the U.S. occupation of the port city of Veracruz for six months.

In the aftermath of the Tampico Affair, the United States became increasingly concerned that instability in Mexico would result in the rise of groups hostile to American interests. Pancho Villa (1878–1923), a Mexican revolutionary general, was initially in good favor with the U.S. government, which at first supported his revolutionary cause. The U.S. government was attracted to Villa because of his political stature as the governor of the Mexican state of Chihuahua. President Wilson, however, chose to side with his rival Venustiano Carranza

(1859–1920), another principle revolutionary leader. Wilson believed that Carranza was the best candidate to expedite the establishment of a stable Mexican government. Carranza became President of Mexico in 1914, replacing the dictatorial Huerta regime. In 1916, President Wilson retaliated against Pancho Villa for a raid that had resulted in the death of 16 American citizens in Columbus, New Mexico. An expeditionary force to Mexico led by U.S. Brigadier General John Pershing (1860–1948) failed to capture Villa.

THE GOOD NEIGHBOR POLICY

In 1933, the administration of President Franklin D. Roosevelt (1882–1945) declared the so-called Good Neighbor policy toward Latin America. This approach effectively reversed the Roosevelt Corollary (introduced by President Theodore Roosevelt in 1904) by renouncing mil-

Doroteo Arango Arámbula, nicknamed Pancho Villa, was the first general of the Mexican Revolution. Despite his numerous exploits, he is remembered today as a folk hero.

itary intervention in the region. Thus, it effectively marked the end of the Banana Wars. During the 1930s, however, the lack of American presence in politically and economically unstable areas opened the way to the rise of a number of dictators, including Fulgencio Batista (1901–1973) in Cuba and Rafael Trujillo (1891–1961) in the Dominican Republic.

The Good Neighbor policy functioned partly because there were already a multitude of regimes that supported American interests. Thus, the United States could maintain influence from the inside rather than from the outside. The FDR administration sought to end the pattern of American intervention in the region that had persisted from 1900 to 1930. For instance, U.S. Marines were sent to Honduras five times from 1905 to 1925 to protect American economic interests or to restore stability. The United States now wanted to maintain a dominant presence in the region, but it did not envision repeated interventions, especially because the American public had become increasingly wary of such entanglements.

Effects of World War

Probably the most important change in U.S. policy in Latin America occurred as a result of geopolitical tensions elsewhere in the world during the first half of the twentieth century. World War I and World War II shifted the American focus toward Europe and Asia and away from Latin America and the Caribbean. The United States gradually shifted its attention back to the region after World War II, resulting in the overthrow of the Jacobo Arbenz (1913–1971) government in Guatemala in 1954, which was inspired by the Central Intelligence Agency. A number of dictators backed by the United States fell shortly after the overthrow of Arbenz, resulting in an increased feeling of anti-Americanism throughout the region. This trend continued in an exceptionally problematic fashion from the U.S. standpoint, as communism grew stronger in the region in the form of the Cuban Revolution (1959).

Bay of Pigs Invasion

The United States remained largely absent in the Caribbean until 1961, when it reengaged with the Bay of Pigs invasion, one the most noteworthy interventions in the history of the region, as

Colonel Carlos Castillo Armash was the rebel leader of the forces that would overthrow Guatemalan President Jacobo Arbenz Guzmán in a military coup. Castillo Armash would later become president of the country and rule until 1957, when he was shot dead in his palace.

it was the lone instance of the United States coming out on the losing side. The invasion was a planned and orchestrated attempt by the U.S. government to overthrow the Communist government of Fidel Castro (1926–), but it failed. It came shortly after John F. Kennedy (1917–1963) had assumed the presidency, and it would play a major role in shaping his foreign-policy decisions. Kennedy was widely criticized over the botched Bay of Pigs invasion, which marked a low point in his presidency. The failed attempt accelerated a rapid deterioration in Cuban-American relations that has persisted to the present day. The Cuban Missile Crisis of October 1962 further solidified popular support for Castro in Cuba and put the two nations even further at odds.

JUSTIFYING U.S. INTERVENTION

The combined aspects of power and proximity largely explain the motivations for American

Fidel Castro's troops successfully repelled the U.S.-backed invasion of the Bay of Pigs.

interventions in Mexico and the Caribbean, particularly as the United States solidified its superpower status through the twentieth century. Through its various interventions, both military and economic, the United States developed a number of relationships throughout the region that enabled it to exert enormous influence both directly and indirectly. U.S. policymakers believed that control of Latin America was in the national interest of the United States. The United States remained during this period more concerned with outside influences on the region than with the internal concerns of the various states in the region. Thus, the United States saw Latin America and the Caribbean as a major component of its sphere of influence and efforts to maintain American hegemony in the Western Hemisphere.

Christopher C. White

GUIDED READING

Eisenhower, John S.D. *Intervention!: The United States and the Mexican Revolution, 1913–1917*. New York: W.W. Norton, 1993.

Langley, Lester. *The Banana Wars: United States Intervention in the Caribbean, 1898–1934*. Lexington: University Press of Kentucky, 1985.

Maingot, Anthony P., and Wilfredo Lozano. *The United States and the Caribbean: Transforming Hegemony and Sovereignty*. New York: Routledge, 2005.

Schoultz, Lars. *Beneath the United States: A History of U.S. Policy Toward Latin America*. Cambridge, MA: Harvard University Press, 1998.

WORLD WAR I

World War I (1914–1919) was the first of a series of devastating global conflicts in the twentieth century that left millions dead and wounded. The war dramatically reshaped world politics through the rise of the United States as a major power and the concurrent disintegration of the Russian, German, and Austro-Hungarian empires.

On the morning of June 28, 1914, Gavrilo Princip (1894–1918), a 19-year-old Serbian nationalist and member of the radical group Young Bosnia, assassinated Austria's Archduke Franz Ferdinand (1863–1914) and his wife, Sophie (1868–1914), in Sarajevo. The assassinations led to war between the Austro-Hungarian Empire and Serbia, and resulted in a domino effect whereby all the major European powers were drawn into war.

A HISTORY OF ALLIANCES

From the end of the Napoleonic Wars in 1815 until World War I, the major European powers of Austria, France, Great Britain, Prussia (later Germany) and Russia had avoided a major war through a series of shifting alliances that came to be known as the Concert of Europe. The five powers would form or dissolve alliances in order to prevent any one country from dominating the others. However, by the end of the nineteenth century, the five empires had been drawn into two rival camps. Austria and Germany were joined in one camp by Italy. The three countries were known as the Triple Alliance (and later the Central Powers). France, Great Britain, and Russia were in the other alliance, referred to as the Triple *Entente*, or "Agreement" (and later, simply as the Allies). Meanwhile, medium-sized and smaller European countries also joined one side or the other, often through secret treaties and agreements.

In line with George Washington's (1732–1799) admonishment to avoid permanent alliances in his Farewell Address and adhering to the tenets of the 1823 Monroe Doctrine, the United States endeavored to avoid being drawn into machinations of either the Concert of Europe or the alliance system that succeeded it.

However, other non-European powers had formal military treaties with European states, including Japan with Great Britain and the Ottoman Empire with Germany.

The Austro-Hungarian Empire declared war on Serbia on July 28, 1914, in response to the assassination, but also as part of a larger pattern of expansion into the Balkans. Russia began mobilizing its forces to support its Serbian ally. In order to preempt an attack on its Austrian ally, Germany, led by Kaiser Wilhelm II (1859–1941), declared war on Russia on August 1. Within a week, France and Great Britain joined the conflict, which drew in other nations as well. Japan declared war on the Central Powers on August 23. The Ottoman Empire declared war on the Allies on October 28. Italy deserted the Central Powers and joined the Allies in the following year. And Bulgaria signed a secret treaty with the Central Powers and also entered the war in 1915.

WILSON ON NEUTRALITY

The noninvolvement policy of the United States toward the war was outlined by President Woodrow Wilson in a message to the Senate on August 19, 1914. In it, Wilson proclaimed the importance of remaining neutral:

"I venture, therefore, my fellow countrymen, to speak a solemn word of warning to you against that deepest, most subtle, most essential breach of neutrality which may spring out of partisanship, out of passionately taking sides. The United States must be neutral in fact, as well as in name, during these days that are to try men's souls. We must be impartial in thought, as well as action, must put a curb upon our sentiments, as well as upon every transaction that might be construed as a preference of one party to the struggle before another."

EARLY BATTLES

When World War I began, German forces invaded France through Belgium, forcing the small, neutral country into the war. The British sent troops across the English Channel to help defend France against Germany. Significant battles took place in the Forest of Ardennes and the frontier region of Alsace-Lorraine in France, as well as along the Belgian frontier. By the end of the year, the German army had advanced deep into France, threatening Paris.

The Germans, however, were stopped, and the war settled into a pattern of trench warfare along the western front, in which both sides built elaborate defensive positions comprised of trenches, tunnels, and barbed wire. Casualties were extensive because the opposing militaries combined nineteenth-century tactics, including massed infantry and cavalry charges, with twentieth-century weapons such as machine guns, artillery, and landmines. At the first Battle of the Marne (September 5–14, 1914), the battle which stopped the German advance on Paris, 263,000 Allied soldiers and more than 250,000 Germans were killed. Later, the opposing sides utilized airplanes, tanks, and even poison gas.

The British military was reinforced with men and materials from other Commonwealth countries, including Australia, New Zealand, Canada, India, and South Africa. In addition, many

Americans crossed into Canada or travelled to France to fight on the side of the Allies. A smaller number of Americans returned to Germany or Austria to volunteer for the Central Powers. The British also launched campaigns against the German colonies in Africa, while both British and Japanese forces attacked German possessions in the Pacific. In 1915, Great Britain and France initiated a series of attacks on the Ottoman Empire. On April 25, 1915, British forces stormed the beaches of Gallipoli in southeast Italy, in a diversionary assault on Turkish troops of the Ottoman Empire. The landing proved disastrous for both sides. British forces, including many Australians and New Zealanders, suffered more than 250,000 casualties, while the Turkish forces had 300,000 casualties. By the end of the year, the war truly had become a global conflict. The United States, China, and Latin America were among the few remaining neutral areas.

In the United States, the population was initially divided over the war. People from the British Isles were the largest immigrant group in the United States and generally supported the Allies. However, many Irish immigrants and their descendents wanted the Central Powers to win because they sought independence for Ireland from Great Britain and hoped the war would weaken the British Empire. Meanwhile, German Americans were the second-largest group in the United States, and their sympathies lay with the Central Powers. American companies sold products and military supplies to both sides, although the majority of U.S. trade occurred with Britain and France. U.S. President Woodrow Wilson (1856–1924) endeavored to maintain American neutrality in the war, but his personal sympathies lay with the Allies due to their democratic nature and because he believed the war resulted from Austrian and German aggression and territorial ambitions.

WAR HITS HOME

At the time, Britain had the world's most powerful navy. Since Germany could not challenge Britain's navy with its own battleships, it turned to submarines. In 1915, Germany began a policy of unrestricted submarine warfare in the waters around Great Britain in an effort to prevent goods and supplies from reaching the island

THE WESTERN FRONT

nation. German submarines committed indiscriminate acts on any ships entering this zone, including those of neutral nations such as the United States. On May 7, 1915, a German submarine sank the British passenger ship *Lusitania* off the coast of Ireland, killing 1,198 passengers and crew, including 128 Americans.

The incident provoked a strong reaction from the Wilson administration. A series of diplomatic notes were sent back and forth between U.S. and German diplomats regarding the sinking of the *Lusitania*. In order to avoid war with the United States, Germany agreed to stop unrestricted submarine warfare. Meanwhile, by the end of the year, Serbia had surrendered to Austria-Hungary, but the stalemate along the western front continued.

In 1916, the Battle of Verdun, in eastern France near the German border, and the Battle of the Somme, in northern France near the Belgian border, exemplified the horrors of trench warfare. At Verdun, more than 750,000 Allied and German soldiers were killed or wounded, while at the Somme there were more than 1 million Allied and German casualties.

Germany again initiated unrestricted submarine warfare in January 1917 after military planners convinced Kaiser Wilhelm II that Britain could be starved into surrender within five months if the submarines cut the islands off from supplies and resources. They argued that even if the United States entered the war, it would be too late, since the British would be out

of the conflict before any U.S. troops could be deployed to Europe.

THE UNITED STATES ENTERS THE WAR

In response to the resumption of unrestricted submarine warfare, the United States cut its diplomatic ties with Germany on February 3, 1917. Fearing war with the United States, German Foreign Minister Arthur Zimmermann sent a secret telegram to the German minister in Mexico. In it, he proposed an alliance between Germany and Mexico. The Germans promised to help the recover territory lost in the Mexican War, including Arizona, New Mexico, and California, if the Mexicans went to war against the United States. British intelligence intercepted the telegram and gave it the United States. Unrestricted submarine warfare and the Zimmermann telegram left the U.S. government with no choice but to declare war on Germany, which it did on April 6, 1917. The recruitment of soldiers began immediately. By June 1917, members of the American Allied Expeditionary Force, under the command of General John J. Pershing, arrived in France, much sooner than the Germans had anticipated. Meanwhile, U.S. naval forces worked with the British against German submarines.

The United States brought fresh troops as well as an economic boost to the Allied Powers. The U.S. government provided loans, food, weapons, and materials to the Allies. The United States also used diplomatic as well as economic

The threat of poison gas attacks created an uneasy existence for soldiers struggling to cope with trench warfare. These French soldiers posing with gas masks in a trench during the Battle of Ypres were faced with the threat of the toxic chlorine and mustard gas.

As war raged in Europe for much of 1916, the United States was in the midst of a presidential election. President Wilson sought reelection against the Republican nominee, Charles Evans Hughes (1862–1948). Wilson emphasized that his administration had kept the country out of the war (his campaign slogan was "He kept us out of war!"). Meanwhile, Hughes urged greater preparedness on the part of the American government and people and criticized Wilson for being weak and indecisive. Wilson's call for neutrality helped him prevail in the election, as many Americans believed that Hughes would lead the country into war. Wilson won 49.2 percent of the vote to the 46.1 percent of Hughes. Nonetheless, Wilson would lead the United States into war six months later.

moved to industrial areas in the north such as Chicago and New York. In addition, as more men were conscripted, an increasing number of women gained employment in industrial jobs or joined the military. These new roles paved the way for woman suffrage after the war.

AMERICAN TROOPS IN EUROPE

The incoming American troops provided a great morale boost for the Allies, whose domestic populations were tired and dispirited by the war. By the end of March 1918, 318,000 U.S. soldiers had crossed the Atlantic to fight against the Central Powers. American efforts to mobilize its soldiers were boosted with the passing of the Selective Services Act (1917), which required that men aged 21 to 30 register for the draft. Another 1 million U.S. troops would arrive in Europe by the end of the summer. By the end of the war, more than half of Americans who had served were draftees.

On March 3, 1918, Russia, economically exhausted and having suffered more than 1.3 million dead or wounded, withdrew from the war through the Treaty of Brest-Litovsk, which it made with the Central Powers. The Russian monarchy had been overthrown by a revolutionary group known as the Bolsheviks, led by Vladimir Lenin (1870–1924), who initiated a Communist government. With its enemy to the east now out of the war, the German army could solely concentrate on the western front. As many as 50 extra German divisions were diverted from the eastern front to the trenches in France.

pressure to convince other, neutral nations to join the conflict. Formerly neutral countries, including China, and many Latin American states, such as Brazil, Costa Rica, and Nicaragua, declared war on the Central Powers. These countries did not provide substantial troops, but they did offer diplomatic and material support to the Allies.

Domestically, the war economy created new jobs and led to large migrations within the United States, especially as Southerners, including significant numbers of African Americans,

The Allied offensive during the fall of 1918 pushed the German army out of France. These American infantry, marching toward the Rhine River during the final weeks of the war, infused a renewed energy in the Allies.

John "Black Jack" Pershing (1860–1948)

John Joseph Pershing was the commander of the American Expeditionary Forces in World War I. Known for his calm demeanor in battle, Pershing had led the African-American troops of the Tenth U.S. Cavalry during the Spanish-American War. His nickname, "Black Jack," resulted from his time commanding African-American forces. Pershing commanded U.S. forces in a 1916 offensive in Mexico in pursuit of Pancho Villa's army. He was respected by many Americans, including former President Theodore Roosevelt, with whom he served during the Spanish-American War. During World War I, the other Allied military commanders looked down on Pershing for what they perceived to be his lack of experience. They sought to divide the American forces and have them serve under British and French commanders. However, Pershing insisted that the U.S. forces remain under a unified command and he proved as able a commander as the best of his British and French counterparts. Many of the most famous U.S. generals of World War II, including George Marshall (1880–1959) and Dwight D. Eisenhower (1890–1969), served under Pershing.

During spring 1918, the German army undertook a series of offensives against the Allied forces. The U.S. Marine Corps fought in France in deeply contested battles in Soissons, Château-Thierry, and Belleau Wood, and helped block German advances toward Paris. Meanwhile, German morale, both at the front and in the homeland, had begun to deteriorate significantly as casualties mounted.

The Final Push

On September 12, 1918, American forces launched the St. Mihiel offensive, south of Verdun, France. American units captured hundreds of German guns and took 13,251 German prisoners. This was the first all-American offensive in World War I. By the end of the month, the Germans had retreated to the Hindenburg Line, where their offensive had begun four years earlier.

In October, the Austro-Hungarian and Ottoman empires collapsed, marking the beginning of the end of the war. The German government began to speak publicly of an armistice, and in early November, Kaiser Wilhelm II abdicated his throne. On November 11, 1918, Germany surrendered.

More than 10 million soldiers perished in World War I, including more than 50,000 American soldiers during their relatively brief but dramatic participation in the war. Wilson was instrumental in the peace process. He wanted to reshape global politics to avoid future world wars through his Fourteen Points proposal. However, the other Allies sought to punish Germany and implemented reparations and other punitive measures, which ultimately would contribute to the outbreak of World War II. The war dramatically altered the political landscape of Europe, with the dissolution of the Austro-Hungarian, German, Ottoman, and Russian empires. The conflict also marked the confirmation of the United States as a major world power.

Gavin Wilk

GUIDED READING

Ferrell, Robert H. *Woodrow Wilson and World War I, 1917–1921.* New York: Harper & Row, 1985.

The Great War and the Shaping of the 20th Century. http://www.pbs.org/greatwar/.

Keegan, John. *The First World War.* New York: Alfred A. Knopf, 1999.

Kennedy, David M. *Over Here: The First World War and American Society.* New York: Oxford University Press, 1980.

Link, Arthur S., ed. *Woodrow Wilson and a Revolutionary World, 1913–1921.* Chapel Hill: University of North Carolina Press, 1982.

Stallings, Laurence. *The Doughboys: The Story of the AEF, 1917–1918.* New York: Harper & Row, 1963.

Strachan, Hew. *The First World War.* New York: Viking, 2004.

CHRONOLOGY

1918

March 3 Russia signs the Treaty of Brest-Litvosk with Germany.

June 3 The Battle of Château-Thierry begins.

June 6 The Battle of Belleau Wood begins.

September 12 St. Mihiel offensive begins.

October 5 The Hindenburg Line is captured by Allied forces.

November 9 Kaiser Wilhelm II abdicates the German throne.

November 11 Armistice is declared, ending World War I.

THE *LUSITANIA* AND SUBMARINE WARFARE

On May 7, 1915, the British passenger ship Lusitania *was sunk by a German submarine off the coast of Ireland. Of 1,959 passengers and crew, 1,198 perished, including 128 American citizens. The attack paved the way for U.S. entry into World War I.*

When World War I began, Great Britain had the most powerful navy in the world. It initiated a blockade of Germany and the other Central Powers, cutting them off from goods and products from neutral countries. Germany attempted to use submarines to offset Britain's naval superiority. Submarines were particularly effective against British merchant vessels. As the war continued, Germany adopted a strategy whereby its submarines would form a blockade around the British Isles and France.

In January 1915, the German government warned the United States that the waters surrounding Great Britain and Ireland were considered war zones and that enemy merchant ships would be attacked without warning. The proclamation was a retaliation aimed at the British naval blockade.

SUBMARINE WARFARE

Under international law at the time, belligerent countries were not supposed to attack merchant ships without warning, and they were not allowed to fire on neutral ships. However, the Germans believed that many British merchant vessels were sailing under the flags of neutral countries and therefore considered them legitimate targets. For example, the Germans had accused William Turner (1856–1933), the captain of the *Lusitania*, of raising a U.S. flag to prevent attacks by German submarines. In addition, there was evidence that the British were using passenger liners to carry arms and munitions, itself a violation of international custom. Finally, the British had also begun arming merchant vessels with deck guns and other armaments that could damage or sink

On the morning of Monday, May 8, 1915, Americans woke up to the front page news that the *Lusitania* had been sunk off the coast of Ireland.

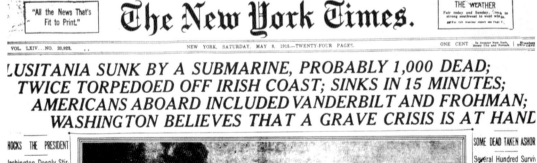

submarines. These factors led to the German decision to attack merchant ships, including passenger ships, without any warning.

In February 1915, as German submarine attacks increased in frequency and intensity, the British initiated countermeasures to disrupt German submarine operations. The British went so far as to construct a series of nets in the Straits of Dover off the southern coast of England that inhibited German submarines from interrupting British shipping. By the second week of April, Winston Churchill (1874–1965), Great Britain's first lord of the admiralty, reported that only 23 ships out of 6,000 arrivals and departures in Great Britain had been sunk by German submarines.

THE FATEFUL ENCOUNTER

As the *Lusitania* left New York on May 1, 1915, the crew and many passengers were aware of danger. The Cunard Steamship Line Shipping Company advertisement of the *Lusitania's* voyages included a notice from the German government warning passengers that ships flying the British flag would be targets of a German attack around the waters of the British Isles. As passengers onboard the *Lusitania* watched the American mainland fade into the distance, the German submarine U-20, captained by Walter Schwieger (1885–1917), headed for the waters off the coast of Liverpool, England. Schwieger guided the submarine around Scotland and Northern Ireland before moving on to the southwest coast of Ireland.

It was in these waters that the *Lusitania* and the German submarine met. The U-20 was returning to Germany when its periscope first sighted the British passenger liner. Captain Schwieger decided against warning the vessel, believing it to be armed. Instead, he ordered a torpedo attack. The *Lusitania* suffered two explosions and sank within 18 minutes.

AFTERMATH OF THE ATTACK

The victims and survivors of the disaster were brought in life rafts to Queenstown, Ireland, as the United States and the rest of the world absorbed the news of the attack on innocent civilians. Calls for an immediate reprisal echoed across the United States, and anti-German propaganda began appearing worldwide. On May 13, in response to the attack, President Woodrow

The sinking of the *Lusitania* precipitated army recruiting posters across Europe in retaliation against the German attack.

Wilson sent the first of three public notes to German Kaiser Wilhelm II, demanding an end to unrestricted submarine warfare. Germany responded to the president's note on May 28, 1915, declaring that the *Lusitania* was a viable, armed target.

Through the diplomatic exchanges, many Americans, including Secretary of State William Jennings Bryan (1860–1925), believed that the Wilson administration was unnecessarily provoking the Germans. Bryan and others argued for a more balanced approach, including demands for concessions from the British, such as an end to the practice of using passenger ships to carry weapons and war supplies. When

THE FIRST NOTE

On May 13, President Wilson wrote his first public note to German Kaiser Wilhelm II, in response to the attack on the *Lusitania*. He stated that the act of unrestricted submarine warfare must be halted:

"The Government of the United States, therefore, desires to call the attention of the Imperial German Government with the utmost earnestness to the fact that the objection to their present method of attack against the trade of their enemies lies in the practical impossibility of employing submarines in the destruction of commerce without disregarding those rules of fairness, reason, justice, and humanity, which all modern opinion regards as imperative."

Wilson refused to mellow the tone of his diplomatic notes to Kaiser Wilhelm II, Bryan resigned.

Wilson's third and final diplomatic note on July 21, 1915, warned Germany that any further belligerent acts upon ships causing harm to American citizens would be considered "deliberately unfriendly." The Germans sought to avoid war with the United States and initially pledged in messages to the American president to return to the previous practice of warning merchant vessels before an attack. Germany also promised not to attack neutral vessels. In August, German submarines were ordered not to attack passenger liners until the crew and passengers had an opportunity to abandon ship.

Strained Relations

Diplomatic posturing continued throughout 1915 and into the following year. Germany realized the impact of tense relations with the United States and limited the scope of its unrestricted warfare. Nevertheless, tensions rose again when, on March 24, 1916, a German submarine torpedoed the French civilian steamship *Sussex* in the English Channel. The German submarine commander believed the *Sussex* was a minelayer, and therefore a legitimate target. This attack occurred without warning, and 80 passengers were killed or injured (including 25 injured Americans). President Wilson threatened to end diplomatic relations, and the German government acquiesced by declaring that no additional merchant and passenger ships would be targeted without warning.

THE END OF DIPLOMACY

On January 17, 1917, the German government again called for unrestricted submarine warfare. Germany reverted back to unrestricted submarine warfare in part because Britain faced a crop failure, and the Germans believed that their submarine fleet could be used to starve Britain into surrender within six months. Two weeks later, the German decision to resume unrestricted submarine warfare was made public. On February 3, the U.S. government severed all diplomatic relations with Germany.

In March, German submarines sank five American freighters, resulting in 36 lives lost. President Wilson could no longer rely on diplomacy to prevent further German attacks. On April 2, 1917, Woodrow Wilson delivered his War Message to Congress. The Senate declared war on April 4, and the House of Representatives echoed that declaration two days later.

Gavin Wilk

GUIDED READING

Hickey, Des, and Gus Smith. *Seven Days to Disaster: The Sinking of the Lusitania.* New York: Putnam, 1982.

The *Lusitania* Resource. http://www.rmslusitania.info.

Peeke, Mitch, Kevin Walsh-Johnson, and Steven Jones. *The Lusitania Story*. Annapolis, MD: Naval Institute, 2002.

Preston, Diana. *Lusitania: An Epic Tragedy.* New York: Walker, 2002.

German submarine attacks on Allied shipping during World War I occurred throughout the Atlantic shipping lanes as well as in the Mediterranean Sea.

THE TREATY OF VERSAILLES AND FOURTEEN POINTS

The Treaty of Versailles (1919) ended World War I. The Fourteen Points, U.S. President Woodrow Wilson's vision for world peace, was offered as the basis for the peace agreement, but the original proposal was significantly altered by the wartime Allies of the United States.

The Fourteen Points were postwar goals promulgated by President Wilson in a speech to Congress on January 8, 1918. Designed to prevent another global war, the Fourteen Points included demands for open covenants of peace (no secret peace treaties), freedom of the seas, fair and equal trade, and disarmament to the minimal levels needed for nations to defend themselves. In addition, they called for foreign troops to be removed from Belgium, Russia, Romania, Serbia, and Montenegro. The Fourteen Points also included the creation of Turkey from the Ottoman Empire, an independent Polish state, and a postwar global organization, the League of Nations, to oversee disputes between countries in order to prevent future wars.

Wilson's Fourteen Points became part of the armistice negotiations between the German government, the Allied Supreme War Council in Paris, and the United States. While Germany agreed to all of its terms, Great Britain and France disagreed with two major elements. The British did not believe in complete freedom of the seas. Instead, they argued that they needed to be able to enact naval blockades during future wars. The French, who had been invaded by Germany and whose land had been ravaged in major battle after major battle, insisted that Germany should be subjected to severe reparations.

On November 11, 1918, the Germans signed an armistice based on a peace settlement encompassing the Fourteen Points. The armistice was a temporary end to the fighting while more formal negotiations were conducted to finalize all aspects of the peace settlement. The Allies believed at the time that any disagreements would be solved once peace negotiations were initiated and a permanent peace treaty was finalized.

NO GRUDGES AGAINST GERMANY

Woodrow Wilson stated his Fourteen Points in a speech to Congress on January 8, 1918. He also spoke of his desire to preserve Germany's stature: *"We have no jealousy of German greatness, and there is nothing in this program that impairs it. We grudge her no achievement or distinction of learning or of pacific enterprise such as have made her record very bright and very enviable. We do not wish to injure her or to block in any way her legitimate influence or power. We do not wish to fight her either with arms or with hostile arrangements of trade if she is willing to associate herself with us and the other peace-loving nations of the world in covenants of justice and law and fair dealing. We wish her only to accept a place of equality among the peoples of the world,—the new world in which we now live,—instead of a place of mastery."*

The world rejoiced on November 11, 1918, as the guns of World War I were finally silenced. These Women's Royal Air Force (WRAF) members were a few of the hundreds of millions that celebrated.

THE PARIS PEACE CONFERENCE

January 18, 1919, marked the first day of the Paris Peace Conference, which took place at the Palace of Versailles just outside of Paris. Five nations (France, Great Britain, the United States, Italy, and Japan) were represented at the outset of the talks, but only France, Great Britain, and the United States—the "Big Three"—formulated the final draft of the Treaty of Versailles (1919). The "Big Four" leaders—British Prime Minster David Lloyd George (1863–1945), French Prime Minster of France Georges Clemenceau (1841–1929), Italian Prime Minister Vittorio Orlando (1860–1952), and U.S. President Wilson—led the conference, but Italy dropped out of the negotiations after its territorial claims to Rijeka, a Croatian seaport, were rejected. Japan also withdrew from the negotiations after refusing to return any of the territory it had acquired in China and the South Pacific during the war. Germany and Austria-Hungary, the principal nations on the losing side, did not actively participate. Negotiations between the Allied leaders and the German delegation would be conducted in writing.

As the negotiations began, it quickly became clear that the Allied Powers had major disagreements. Two issues, reparations and territory, dominated the discussions. France would not waver in its determination that Germany pay large reparations to cover the costs of the war. In addition, France wanted Germany to lose large swaths of territory so that it could not threaten the rest of Europe. Among the Fourteen Points was a call that areas lost to Germany in the 1871 Franco-Prussian War be returned to French sovereignty, but France wanted to create a larger buffer between itself and Germany. As the months passed, the original Fourteen Points that began as the centerpiece of the armistice had been largely eroded. In early May 1919, the Allied leaders agreed on the terms of the final treaty.

German Disapproval

On May 7, 1919, the Allies handed over the peace terms to the German delegation and gave it two weeks to respond. As the German diplomats began scouring the pages of the treaty, they were shocked at the details.

The Germans responded with a counterproposal. They complained that the terms of the draft treaty demanded exorbitant reparations and eliminated some aspects of their national sovereignty, including dramatic reductions in the German military and the loss of territory. For instance, Poland was created through the transfer of large pieces of German territory (other territory was transferred or returned to Belgium, Czechoslovakia, Denmark, France and Lithuania). The Allies had succeeded in convincing the United States to allow the French to occupy the industrial Saar region, the Rhineland

The "Big Four" leaders gathered at Versailles. From left, Italian Prime Minister Orlando, French Prime Minister Clemenceau, British Prime Minster Lloyd George, and U.S. President Wilson.

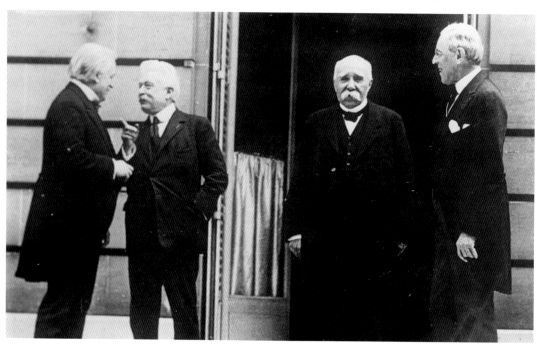

and parts of Bavaria, in Germany, for 15 years. All the coal produced in the rich Saar region would be shipped to France. Germany had to also surrender its overseas colonies. In addition, the delegates were dismayed that the German merchant fleet would be eliminated and that Germany would be excluded from the proposed League of Nations.

Compromise

The British delegation began to express trepidation with the draft treaty, fearing that the terms might be too harsh on the Germans and foster undue animosity in the German government and general population. British Prime Minister Lloyd George did gain one concession regarding Upper Silesia, part of the region designated for Poland; residents of the area would decide by a vote whether to remain part of Germany or be incorporated into Poland. The terms of the treaty regarding reparations would not be changed, however, charging the German regime a total of approximately $33 billion. Included in this total was the cost of occupation that the Allies charged to Germany, 10 years of free coal and iron that would be transferred to France and Belgium, and the surrender of large merchant ships from Germany to the allies. Article 231 of the treaty forced Germany to accept guilt for starting the war, and Germany lost about 13 percent of its territory and 6 million citizens. The German army was limited to 100,000 troops, and it was not allowed to possess tanks or heavy artillery. The German navy was also given strict limitations on size and the number of ships and the country was not allowed to have an air force.

THE TREATY OF VERSAILLES

The revised treaty was handed to the German delegation on June 16, and the delegates were given three days to accept its terms. After serious deliberations, the German government reluctantly accepted the terms of the document, and the Treaty of Versailles was signed on June 28, 1919. Allied celebrations followed, but many Germans believed that their country was being unfairly punished. By the mid-1920s, a number of German nationalist groups, including the Nazi Party, had gained popularity because of their opposition to the terms of the Treaty of Versailles.

On July 8, a crowd of 100,000 people gathered to cheer President Wilson upon his return to Washington, D.C. Two days later, he presented the terms of the Treaty of Versailles to the U.S. Congress, along with a proposal that the United States enter the League of Nations.

As the congressional debates over the Treaty of Versailles and the League of Nations turned from weeks to months, it became increasingly clear that the president did not have the support of the Senate. During fall 1919, President Wilson received the Nobel Peace Prize, but also suffered a stroke in October. Ultimately, the U.S. Senate, led by Henry Cabot Lodge, rejected the Treaty of Versailles in a vote of 35 against and 49 in favor (seven votes short of the necessary two-thirds majority to ratify the treaty). It marked the first time in U.S. history that the Senate did not ratify a peace agreement. Opposition to the treaty was caused by the traditional isolationism of many Americans, who opposed membership in the League of Nations, and by Wilson's unwillingness to compromise with senators who sought to include language in the treaty that would protect U.S. sovereignty by limiting the powers of the League of Nations. The United States never joined the League of Nations, which dramatically undermined the effectiveness of the organization.

Gavin Wilk

Senator Henry Cabot Lodge was the main opponent to the Treaty of Versailles and American involvement in the League of Nations.

GUIDED READING

Birdsall, Paul. *Versailles Twenty Years After*. Hamden, CT: Archon, 1962.

League of Nations Photo Archive. http://www. indiana.edu/~league/.

MacMillan, Margaret. *Paris 1919: Six Months that Changed the World*. New York: Random House, 2002.

THE LEAGUE OF NATIONS AND ISOLATIONISM

In the aftermath of World War I, President Woodrow Wilson attempted to bring the United States into the newly formed League of Nations, but isolationist opposition in the U.S. Senate, in addition to Wilson's own refusal to compromise, prevented U.S. membership.

In January 1919, President Wilson traveled to the Paris Peace Conference at Versailles with his second wife, Edith.

After World War I, public opinion in France and Great Britain favored harsh punishment for Germany. Both French Prime Minister Georges Clemenceau and British Prime Minister David Lloyd George officially adopted positions reflecting public opinion in their respective nations. Privately, however, Lloyd George favored less punitive measures, as he thought it was important to maintain a balance of power in Europe. If Germany were too harshly punished, he reasoned, then France would be the only great power remaining on the continent—a prospect that might threaten British colonial interests and lead to further conflict. Wilson took the least punitive position of the Big Three leaders and brought to the table his famous Fourteen Points plan for peace. Among the most controversial of Wilson's Fourteen Points was the call for an international association, the League of Nations, to promote world peace.

In the end, the Treaty of Versailles demanded, among other things, that Germany relinquish its colonial possessions, reduce its military capacity, and pay reparations. While the treaty did endorse the League of Nations, it did not agree to a universal right of self-determination for subject nations, a right that France and Britain regarded as a threat to their colonial dominions.

It was assumed in Europe that the United States would play a leading role in the League of Nations, but President Wilson faced stiff opposition from congressional isolationists who feared that involvement in the League would draw the United States into foreign wars that did not serve the best national interest.

WILSON AND THE SENATE: THE LEAGUE OF NATIONS DEBATE

When Wilson returned from France to the United States in early 1919, he was faced with the task of obtaining Senate ratification of the

THE ISOLATIONIST TRADITION

The term *isolationism* describes an attitude toward involvement in foreign affairs prevalent in the United States since its founding. Isolationists do not support complete isolation. Instead, they believe that the United States, as a democratic, trading nation, should, in its own interest, develop extensive diplomatic and commercial ties with the nations of the world. Isolationists, however, oppose the establishment of treaties and alliances that involve the United States in foreign conflicts that serve no genuine American interest. This position was adopted by the British (and later American) revolutionary Thomas Paine (1737–1809) in his book *Common Sense*, an influential work during and after the American Revolution. The same position was voiced by George Washington (1732–1799) in his Farewell Address of 1796. Thomas Jefferson (1743–1826), in his first inaugural address in 1801, reiterated the position succinctly when he called for "Peace, commerce, and honest friendship with all nations—entangling alliances with none." During the century prior to World War I, isolationism was the predominant attitude in American foreign policy. At the outset of the war, Americans overwhelmingly believed that the conflict was a European affair and insisted on maintaining a position of neutrality. This was, in fact, the position of President Wilson himself. The refusal to take sides persisted until attacks by German submarines against American merchant ships tipped the scales in favor of involvement.

Treaty of Versailles. Because the treaty endorsed the controversial formation of a League of Nations, debate over ratification dragged on for months. Initially, public opinion favored the League of Nations, and Wilson's own party, the Democrats, solidly supported the idea. Many Republicans also supported the League, though with reservations. Nevertheless, a powerful minority of 14 Senate Republicans known as the irreconcilables, most of them isolationists, were unwilling to accept U.S. entry into the League of Nations. The irreconcilables were led by Idaho Senator William Borah (1865–1940), a member of the Foreign Relations Committee. Because the treaty was required to pass through his committee before being debated on the open Senate floor, Borah was positioned perfectly to obstruct passage.

Borah and the irreconcilables objected most strenuously to Article 10 of the League of Nations covenant, which committed individual member states "to respect and preserve ... against external aggression the territorial integrity and existing independence of all members of the League." This stipulation, in the view of the isolationists, seemed to commit the United States to military intervention anyplace in the world where another member nation's sovereignty might be threatened.

As the Senate debate dragged on, American public opinion began to vacillate. By the time the treaty passed through the hands of the Foreign Relations Committee, numerous reservations had been attached and approved by Senate Majority Leader Henry Cabot Lodge (1850–1924), one of which sought to make any U.S. military action taken under the auspices of Article 10 subject to congressional approval. Lodge, a senior Republican senator representing Massachusetts, staunchly opposed the United States entering into any binding international agreements with other nations.

As the Treaty of Versailles was debated on the Senate floor during the fall of 1919, Wilson and his supporters repeatedly refused to compromise. The final vote on the treaty in November failed to achieve the two-thirds majority required for ratification, and U.S. entry into the League of Nations was thus prevented. Most historians agree that had Wilson shown some willingness to compromise with isolationist reservations, the treaty would have been approved. However, the League of Nations had largely been Wilson's own inspiration, and he had a great deal of personal pride invested in its success. He had composed Article 10 of the League Covenants himself, and, unlike the irreconcilables, he did not believe that it posed any

WILLIAM BORAH'S SENATE ADDRESS

During the months of debate over the Versailles Treaty, Senator Borah, a Republican from Idaho, spoke often before the Foreign Relations Committee and the public-at-large. A master orator, he frequently was quoted by the press. His message, which he hammered home relentlessly, was that U.S. involvement in the League of Nations would compromise American sovereignty. It is widely agreed that his eloquence helped to sway public opinion and to solidify opposition to the Treaty of Versailles in the Senate. On the day of the final vote, November 19, 1919, Borah delivered a major address on the Senate floor. At the climax of his speech, responding to critics who had argued that the isolationists were too narrow in their view of the national interest, he proclaimed:

"Since the debate opened months ago, those of us who have stood against this proposition have been taunted many times with being little Americans. Leave us the word American ... and no taunt can disturb us, no gibe discompose our purposes. ... We have sought nothing save the tranquility of our own people and the honor and independence of our own Republic. No foreign flattery, no possible world glory and power have disturbed our poise or come between us and our devotion to the traditions which have made us a people or the policies which have made us a Nation."

threat to national sovereignty. In his view, Article 10 was essential to ensuring the success of the League of Nations.

FOREIGN POLICY AND THE LEAGUE AFTER 1919

Although the United States never joined, the League of Nations became a short-lived experiment in international cooperation. It was dissolved in 1946 at the conclusion of World War II, in part because it had failed in its primary mission to avert another world war. The League of Nations did achieve some notable victories. For example, under the auspices of the International Labor Organization (ILO), a League agency, working conditions for laborers were improved in a number of countries. Slave labor was eliminated in some notable instances, such as in Sierra Leone, where 200,000 forced laborers were freed in 1927.

As an arbitrator of disputes between sovereign nation-states, the League did achieve a few successes prior to 1930. In a 1921 dispute between Germany and Poland over Upper Silesia, the League brokered a peaceful agreement to split the territory. However, its efforts were largely ineffective in the few significant military conflicts in which it did intervene. Japan invaded Manchuria in 1932, drove out the Chinese, and set up a new government. After a long delay, the League ordered Japan out of Manchuria in 1933, but the Japanese government simply ignored the order. One major reason for this was that the League had no independent military force with

which to back up its directives. It depended entirely upon the willingness of a handful of permanent members, most of which were major European powers, to place their military force at the disposal of the League. In the case of Manchuria, European powers such as Great Britain were reluctant to become involved. All too often, the League's permanent members were unwilling to sacrifice their own strategic interests for the sake of collective interests.

Jack Trotter

GUIDED READING

Bailey, Thomas A. *Woodrow Wilson and the Great Betrayal.* New York: Macmillan, 1945.

Byrd, Robert C. *The Senate, 1789–1989.* Washington, DC: U.S. Government Printing Office, 1994.

Cooper, John Milton. *The Vanity of Power: American Isolationism and the First World War 1914–1917.* Westport, CT: Greenwood, 1969.

Maddox, Robert James. *William E. Borah and American Foreign Policy.* Baton Rouge: Louisiana State University Press, 1969.

Miller, Karen A.J. *Populist Nationalism: Republican Insurgency and American Foreign Policy Making, 1918–1925.* Westport, CT: Greenwood, 1999.

THE FIRST RED SCARE

Revolutions abroad and anarchist activities at home provoked a backlash against radical political activity in the United States in the late 1910s and early 1920s that fueled American isolationism and affected U.S. foreign policy after World War I.

From its inception, the United States was a destination for millions of immigrants from many nations and diverse ethnic backgrounds. A policy of virtually unrestricted immigration facilitated this massive influx, which brought approximately 35 million people to the United States during the nineteenth century. Immigration often prompted negative reactions from those with established citizenship, particularly against newcomers whose languages, cultures, and physical characteristics differed from those of the majority.

Global turmoil during the early twentieth century, including World War I, aroused fears of radical political activity among particular groups of immigrants in the United States and other Western nations. Although the activities of Marxists and anarchists, both of whom advocated the overthrow of Western capitalist societies, had resulted in violence and uprisings in some European nations during the late nineteenth century, there was little evidence of such activity within U.S. borders during this period. At the outset of the twentieth century, however, isolated acts of violence by lone anarchists and radical groups on the fringes of the organized labor movement occurred in the United States. Most notably, President William McKinley (1843–1901) was assassinated in 1901 by a self-proclaimed anarchist. Ten years later, a series of violent acts perpetrated by followers of anarchist leader Luigi Galleani (1861–1931) sparked American fears of radicalism and subversive activities among immigrant populations, which comprised much of the labor force.

REVOLUTION AND REACTION

The emergence of communism as a global political force exacerbated fears of external threats to peace and stability in the Western world. In October 1917, a Communist revolution occurred in Russia when the Bolshevik Party overthrew the czarist government. The

Bolsheviks proclaimed that the takeover was the initial phase of an international revolution in which workers all over the world would unite and create a stateless, global society. The establishment in March 1919 of the Communist International, or Comintern, led by the Bolsheviks, and the subsequent establishment of the Communist Party throughout Europe, Latin America, Australia, and the Middle East during the late 1910s and early 1920s, seemed to validate the possibility of global revolution. Labor unrest in Great Britain, Spain, and France sparked concern that Bolshevism would spread in the Western world. But nowhere were fears of Communist revolution so great as in the United States, where anti-Communist hysteria took hold—despite scant evidence of Communist activity within its borders. News of Russia's

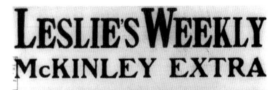

An illustration of President William McKinley's imprisoned assassin, Leon F. Czolgosz, appeared in a September 9, 1901, edition of *Leslie's Weekly.*

Bolshevik Revolution, coupled with escalating labor unrest that resulted in a series of strikes in 1918 and 1919, prompted many Americans to equate the activities of disparate radical groups with Bolshevism.

The legal mechanisms used to suppress incidents of radical political activity during the first Red Scare were designed prior to U.S. entry into World War I. Their purpose was to quell political dissent and galvanize support for the war effort. In 1917, Congress had passed the Espionage Act, a sweeping piece of legislation that made illegal any action that could be perceived as interfering with the operation of the U.S. military. In 1918, Congress passed the Sedition Act, which forbade speech that could be deemed "disloyal" to the government, the flag, or the military. Both acts were used to suppress a variety of political activities. The U.S. Post Office, for example, refused to deliver publications deemed subversive, including literature distributed by Galleani and his followers. Anarchists and German Americans were the primary targets of the new laws, the enforcement of which slowed toward the end of World War I, only to be resurrected following the Bolshevik Revolution.

HEIGHT OF THE RED SCARE

The Red Scare began in earnest after a series of bombings and attempted bombings from April through June 1919, in which at least 30 prominent government officials and businessmen were targeted, including U.S. Attorney General A. Mitchell Palmer (1872–1936). Most of the bombs were sent by mail and intercepted before reaching their intended destinations, but several people were injured and at least one person was killed. On June 2, 1919, a suicide bomber blew himself up in front of the home of Attorney General Palmer, damaging the home but failing to injure Palmer. Nearly all of the bombings were traced to followers of Galleani.

The government's response to the attacks was swift and massive. President Woodrow Wilson ordered Attorney General Palmer to take action, and Congress followed suit by dramatically increasing the budget for the attorney general's office and the Bureau of Investigation (the forerunner of the Federal Bureau of Investigation). The two agencies then carried out a series of actions known as the Palmer Raids, which resulted in the arrest of more than 10,000 individuals. It also led to the deportation of hundreds of resident aliens, including Galleani, under provisions of the Espionage and Sedition acts. Many prominent Americans called for more deportations, mass imprisonments, and even executions of persons with radical beliefs.

Antiradical and anti-immigrant sentiments intensified in the early 1920s, as communism continued to make inroads abroad and anarchist

Passersby observe the aftermath of an anarchist bombing on Wall Street, New York City, in 1920.

attacks continued in the United States. On September 16, 1920, the bombing of an office building on Wall Street in New York City, which killed 38 people and injured an additional 400, was traced to followers of Galleani. That same year, two other Italian anarchists, Nicola Sacco (1891–1927) and Bartolomeo Vanzetti (1888–1927), were arrested for armed robbery and murder in Massachusetts. The two immigrant laborers were subsequently convicted, despite weak evidence, and executed in 1927 amid a massive public outcry. The executions became symbolic of the excesses of the first Red Scare.

IMPACT

The ramifications of the first Red Scare were far-reaching and enduring. Fear of revolutionary ideas contributed to a shift toward isolationism on the part of the American people and government. This led to the failure of the United States to participate in the League of Nations and prompted a reluctance to cooperate with the Allies in confronting the political and economic conditions that led to the outbreak of World War II. The Red Scare also contributed to government policies limiting immigration in the 1920s, which provoked anti-American sentiments in various foreign countries. Domestically, government reactions to the Red Scare set a precedent for repressive bureaucratic action in times of national crisis, echoed in the second Red Scare of the 1940s and 1950s.

Michael H. Burchett

GUIDED READING

Avrich, Paul. *Sacco and Vanzetti: The Anarchist Background*, Princeton, NJ: Princeton University Press, 1991.

Feuerlicht, Roberta Strauss. *America's Reign of Terror: World War I, the Red Scare, and the Palmer Raids*. New York: Random House, 1971.

Preston, William, Jr. *Aliens and Dissenters: Federal Suppression of Radicals, 1903–1933*. Urbana: University of Illinois Press, 1994.

Read, Anthony. *The World on Fire: 1919 and the Battle with Bolshevism*. New York: W.W. Norton, 2008.

Italian anarchists Nicola Sacco (*right*) and Bartolomeo Vanzetti (*left*) are pictured after their arrest on charges of murder in 1920.

CONSPIRACY AGAINST DEMOCRACY

An article titled "The Case Against the Reds," by U.S. Attorney General A. Mitchell Palmer in 1920, illustrates the manner in which communism, anarchism, and organized labor were portrayed as a single global conspiracy against democracy and order during the first Red Scare:

"Like a prairie-fire, the blaze of revolution was sweeping over every American institution of law and order a year ago. It was eating its way into the homes of the American workmen, its sharp tongues of revolutionary heat were licking the altars of the churches, leaping into the belfry of the school bell, crawling into the sacred corners of American homes, seeking to replace marriage vows with libertine laws, burning up the foundations of society. Robbery, not war, is the ideal of communism. This has been demonstrated in Russia, Germany, and in America. As a foe, the anarchist is fearless of his own life, for his creed is a fanaticism that admits no respect of any other creed. Obviously it is the creed of any criminal mind."

THE GLOBAL GREAT DEPRESSION

During the 1920s, overproduction and an unsustainable cycle of inflation and debt combined to produce economic instability in Europe. Heavily dependent on the American economy for loans and trade, European nations followed the United States into economic decline during the late 1920s and early 1930s. The result was a global economic downturn of unprecedented proportions.

These boys in famine-stricken post–World War I Austria walk home with firewood gathered in the Brennholz, located some 15 miles (24 kilometers) from Vienna.

The causes of the global Great Depression were numerous and varied, difficult even for economists to pinpoint or quantify. They have been the source of subsequent debate among generations of scholars. A significant cause was the economic turmoil that prevailed in many European countries following World War I. The enormous cost of war incurred by European nations had led many of them to increase their supply of money, which resulted in inflation.

Defeated nations, most notably Germany, were forced to pay enormous reparations to the victorious Allied Powers. This led Germany to increase its money supply as well as borrow money to satisfy these debts. Later, efforts to control inflation by reining in money supplies and artificially returning prices to prewar levels led to further instability.

In an effort to control currency instability in Europe, the U.S. government implemented the Dawes Plan (1924), named after its author, political advisor and government administrator Charles G. Dawes (1865–1951). The plan called for extending loans to Germany that the country would then use to pay its war debts to the European Allied Powers, which in turn would pay their own debts to the United States. The Dawes Plan, while temporarily stabilizing the European economy, also made the state of global economics more dependent on the health of the American economy.

END OF THE BOOM

In the United States, rapid economic growth during the "roaring twenties" led to overproduction of manufactured and agricultural goods.

Factories produced more goods and realized more profits than ever; yet wages increased little for rank-and-file workers, and declining prices for crops and livestock meant that farmers produced more food for less money. As a result, the gap between rich and poor increased, and many Americans could not afford to buy the same goods they produced. An increase in consumer credit had allowed many of these consumers to purchase big-ticket items on installment plans, adding further incentive for manufacturers to overproduce goods. The rapid growth of manufacturing resulted in many companies becoming overvalued on the stock market.

By the late 1920s, rising prices and static wages had forced working Americans to cut personal spending, which drastically decreased both the demand for manufactured goods and the profits of manufacturers. The value of stock in many companies plunged, culminating in the great stock market crash of October 1929. A large number of debtors subsequently defaulted on the debts they owed to banks. As a result, many banks simply failed, closing their doors as people rushed to withdraw their savings. By 1932, defaults on loans to farms and businesses had resulted in the collapse of more than 5,000 banks.

THE DEPRESSION GOES GLOBAL

Economic turmoil in the United States added to the distress of European companies, which relied heavily on international trade to support their economies. In 1930, in a desperate attempt to promote consumption of American-made products, the U.S. Congress enacted the Hawley-Smoot Tariff Act, which sharply increased duties on imported goods. The move further fueled the economic decline of European nations already struggling to industrialize in the face of mounting debt. Many European nations responded to the tariff act by themselves raising tariffs on American goods, harming the U.S. manufacturers and farmers that Hawley-Smoot

Unemployed men lined up for coffee and bread at a soup kitchen run by the Bahai Fellowship in New York, circa 1930.

was meant to protect—and reversing trends that appeared to mark the beginnings of a natural recovery in the global economy. Nations dependent on international trade to support their economies began defaulting on their loans, leading to more turmoil in the banking industry.

Throughout the 1930s, the devastating effects of economic depression rippled throughout the markets of the industrialized world. Unemployment soared as international trade nearly ground to a halt—millions of jobs disappeared as the economy contracted and at the height of the Great Depression in 1932. Unemployment reached 25 percent in the United States and Great Britain, nearly 33 percent in Australia, and 40 percent in Germany. Farmers and unskilled workers were the hardest hit. Millions of them wandered the countryside as refugees, seeking shelter and sustenance wherever they could find it.

Economic hardship led many Europeans to embrace political ideologies such as communism or extreme nationalism, and some sought scapegoats to blame for their problems. In Germany, troubled economic times contributed to the emergence of the Nazi Party, whose leader, Adolf Hitler (1889–1945), seized power and established an oppressive, militaristic regime that conquered much of western Europe

throughout the 1930s, ultimately triggering World War II. Fascist movements also thrived in Latin America, where national economies supported by heavy American investment were devastated.

In 1931, with the West distracted by economic woes, Japan took the opportunity to launch an invasion of Manchuria, a region in northern China. The United States unsuccessfully attempted a passive solution by adopting a policy of nonrecognition, outlined in the Stimson Doctrine (1932), named for Secretary of State Henry L. Stimson (1867–1950). European powers organized under the League of Nations echoed U.S. attempts at stemming the conflict through diplomacy, but failed to act against the Japanese when the United States—holding firmly to its policy of isolationism—refused to support a forceful retaliation.

A SLOW RESPONSE

In the tradition of individualism, which discouraged government interference in the free market, U.S. President Herbert Hoover (1874–1964) echoed the belief of many international government and industrial leaders that the American economy was experiencing a cyclical downturn and would correct itself naturally. But at the height of the Great Depression, Americans, like many Europeans, demanded drastic government action to reverse the causes and effects of economic collapse. They elected a new president—Franklin D. Roosevelt—who took office in 1933 and initiated a series of sweeping public policy measures known as the New Deal. But because the U.S. government maintained the isolationist stance it had assumed following World War I, American efforts to help the rest of the world were limited in scope and effectiveness.

As a result of Roosevelt's New Deal programs, the U.S. economy slowly recovered during the 1930s, but did not fully emerge from the Great Depression until World War II revived American industry in the 1940s. While the United States enjoyed a long period of postwar economic expansion, the combined effects of the global depression and war exacted a catastrophic toll on European nations. Many European countries did not begin to experience significant economic growth until well into the latter half of the twentieth century.

Michael H. Burchett

Popular unrest resulting from the Great Depression aided the rise of Adolf Hitler to power in Germany.

SUPPORT VS. NO SUPPORT

U.S. President Herbert Hoover resisted calls for government intervention during the economic crisis.
In a press statement from 1931, Hoover cited the words of President Grover Cleveland, who, in
vetoing a bill to provide seed money to drought-stricken farmers in 1887, stated:
*"[T]he lesson should be constantly enforced that though the people support the
Government the Government [sic.] should not support the people."*

By contrast, Franklin D. Roosevelt called for immediate and aggressive
government intervention in his first inaugural address, declaring that:
*"Our greatest primary task is to put people to work ... accomplishing greatly needed projects to
stimulate and reorganize the use of our national resources. ... There are many ways in which it
[putting people to work] can be helped, but it can never be helped merely by talking about it.
We must act, and act quickly."*

Franklin Delano Roosevelt makes his first inaugural address in 1933 as the thirty-second president of the United States. Beneath him in the photo is the American symbol of an eagle with its wings spread. Roosevelt was the only president to win four consecutive terms.

GUIDED READING

Feinstein, Charles H. *The European Economy Between the Wars*. New York: Oxford University Press, 1997.

Houck, Davis W. *FDR and Fear Itself: The First Inaugural Address*. College Station: Texas A&M University Press, 2002.

McElvaine, Robert S. *The Great Depression: America 1929–1941*. New York: Times Books, 1993.

Rothermund, Dietmar. *The Global Impact of the Great Depression, 1929–1939*. New York: Routledge, 1996.

TARIFFS, PROTECTIONISM, AND THE INTERNATIONAL ECONOMY

The global Great Depression was exacerbated by the adoption of high tariffs in many countries, starting with the United States. The tariffs were the most concrete manifestation of a resurging philosophy of economic protectionism, which held that a country's domestic industries must be protected from foreign competition.

Since the eighteenth century, policy makers have debated the relative merits of economic protectionism and free trade. Protectionism is the modern equivalent of the mercantilist system of the seventeenth and eighteenth centuries. Protectionists believe that a nation becomes more prosperous by running a trade surplus, and that governments ought to take positive steps to ensure such an outcome. Historically, the most widely employed protectionist measure has been the protective tariff, a tax designed to shelter favored producers (usually manufacturers) from foreign competition.

The opposite of protectionism is free trade, a philosophy advocated most famously in Adam Smith's (1723–1790) classic text on free-market economics, *The Wealth of Nations* (1776). According to this view, national prosperity comes from the development of—and increase in—the division of labor, and that foreign trade furthers that process by allowing greater economic specialization and efficiency. Free traders favor tariffs only for revenue purposes, if at all. Today, most economists favor the free trade position.

PROTECTIONISM VS. FREE TRADE IN U.S. HISTORY

Early in the history of the United States, the opposing philosophies of protectionism and free trade were articulated by Alexander Hamilton (1755–1804), who argued for protectionism, and Thomas Jefferson (1743–1826), who supported free trade. Free traders held the upper hand in national politics during the first half of the nineteenth century, but protectionists came into power after the Southern states seceded in 1861. During the Gilded Age, the post-Reconstruction era characterized by material wealth and politi-

cal corruption, tariffs were a major issue dividing Republicans (protectionists) from Democrats (free traders). However, Republican dominance in Congress and the presidency from 1861 until 1912 was reflected in generally high tariffs. Tariffs fell in President Woodrow Wilson's first term and remained relatively low throughout the 1920s.

Alexander Hamilton was the foremost proponent of protectionism in the generation after American independence. His intellectual heirs have argued ever since for protective tariffs and heavy regulation of foreign trade.

Tariffs were not a significant issue in the 1928 presidential election, although Republican Herbert Hoover indicated that he would welcome a more protectionist policy. Following Hoover's victory, Congress held hearings on implementing tariffs, which produced more than 20,000 pages of testimony, most of it from interest groups lobbying for protection for their products. The result of these hearings was the Hawley-Smoot Tariff Act (1930), named for its Republican sponsors in Congress: Representative Willis C. Hawley (1864–1941) and Senator Reed Smoot (1862–1941). Hoover had pushed for higher duties on agricultural products, believing that these would help farmers whose exports had been declining as European agriculture recovered in the wake of World War I. However, intense lobbying from interest groups led to the Hawley-Smoot Tariff bill, which called for raising duties on a wide range of both agricultural and manufactured goods—increases averaging 59 percent on over 25,000 items. More than 1,000 economists signed a petition asking Hoover to veto the bill, and industrialist Henry Ford (1863–1947) spent an evening at the White House arguing against the measure. Nevertheless, Hoover signed the tariff act on June 17, 1930.

In anticipation of a worldwide surge in protectionism, the U.S. stock market broke sharply the day Hoover announced his intention to sign the Hawley-Smoot Tariff Act, and it continued to decline in the succeeding months. Nearly every significant trading partner of the United States experienced economic dislocation in important industries as a result of the new tariffs. For example, Canadian producers of dairy products, fish, potatoes, cattle, wheat, apples, and lumber all suffered from the hike in rates. The almost universal response from U.S. trading partners was the implementation of retaliatory tariffs directed against U.S. exporters. Spain, angered over Smoot-Hawley's exclusion of cork, increased its tariff on American automobiles by 150 percent. Italy, harmed by the tariff act's treatment of copper, wheat, cotton, and leather, doubled its tariff on American automobiles and increased the duty on American radios by 500 percent. France established import quotas that shut many American goods out of its market. Other countries in Europe and the Americas took similar measures.

By 1934, international trade worldwide had fallen to one-third its 1929 level. This development threatened the repayment to the United States of European debts dating from World War I. Countries such as Great Britain and France relied on proceeds from their exports to the United States, which had fallen by roughly 75 percent, to service their debt payments. U.S. farmers, whom Hoover intended to be the principal beneficiaries of the Smoot-Hawley tariff, saw their export markets collapse because foreign trading partners did not have the foreign exchange reserves necessary to purchase U.S. agricultural commodities. Simultaneously, the tariff forced U.S. farmers to pay higher prices for manufactured goods. Agricultural and manufacturing workers who lost their jobs because of falling exports often found it difficult or impossible to find new work in the rigid labor environment brought about by the Hoover and Roosevelt administrations' new regulations, such as wage and price floors.

The tariff regime of the 1930s also contributed to a tendency toward domestic monopolies in various industries. By limiting consumer choice and permitting domestic producers to charge rates above the world market price, the tariff resulted in an anti-competitive

Industrialist Henry Ford was one of the American businessmen most harmed by the Smoot-Hawley Tariff. Many foreign governments retaliated against American protectionism by imposing steep tariffs on American automobiles, thereby crippling Ford's international sales.

On December 7, 1929, Senator Smoot and Representative Hawley pose behind boxes full of petitions from interest groups around the country requesting protective tariffs for products in their industries.

environment at odds with the government's nominal antitrust policy. The Communications Act (1934), which created the Federal Communications Commission, and other antitrust legislation of the 1930s may not have been necessary in the absence of high tariffs.

REFLECTIONS ON THE SMOOT-HAWLEY TARIFF

In 1944, Sumner Welles (1892–1961), who served as Franklin D. Roosevelt's undersecretary of state, published a book called *The Time or Decision*, which contained both a review of recent diplomatic history and a series of proposals for postwar Europe. In it, Welles offered the following assessment of the impact of the Smoot-Hawley tariff:

"The high tariff rolled up unemployment in Great Britain and western Europe. [It] encouraged the German government to adopt its autarchic economic policy, which in turn was a contributing factor in bringing about the second World War."

During his first two terms as president, Roosevelt and Congress did little to ameliorate trade conditions. In 1934, the Reciprocal Trade Agreements Act was passed, which permitted the president to negotiate tariff-reduction agreements with foreign countries. Theoretically, duties could be lowered by up to 50 percent under the legislation, but only a handful of deals were concluded during the 1930s, and the average rate reduction was just 4 percent.

IMPACT

The overall impact of protectionism on the Great Depression remains in dispute among economists and economic historians. The majority opinion is that it was an exacerbating factor, but not the root cause. There is little doubt that protectionism damaged the international division of labor and artificially directed productive energies into relatively inefficient lines of production. Substantial trade liberalization did not occur until after World War II, once the philosophical argument for free trade once again became widely accepted among world leaders.

Jason E. Jewell

GUIDED READING

Jones, Joseph M. *Tariff Retaliation: Repercussions of the Hawley-Smoot Bill.* Philadelphia: University of Pennsylvania Press, 1934.

Kindleberger, Charles P. *The World in Depression, 1929–1939.* Berkeley: University of California Press, 1986.

Pierce, Franklin. *The Tariff and the Trusts.* New York: Macmillan, 1913.

Powell, Jim. *FDR's Folly: How Roosevelt and his New Deal Prolonged the Great Depression.* New York: Crown Forum, 2003.

Rothbard, Murray N. *America's Great Depression.* Auburn, AL: Mises Institute, 2000.

WOMAN SUFFRAGE AT HOME AND ABROAD

In the late 1800s, women's rights groups on both sides of the Atlantic won voting rights at the local level, but it was not until the early twentieth century, as a result of more assertive tactics and the circumstances wrought by World War I, that women in Europe and the Americas gained suffrage at the national level.

For millennia, women were excluded from the political sphere and, apart from the exceptional monarch, were without political power. During the medieval period, European women had rights as nobles, but those rights were related to property rather than politics. During the French and American revolutions of the late 1700s, women's voting rights were debated but denied. In France, however, revolutionaries questioned gender inequality more than American revolutionaries did.

REPUBLICAN MOTHERS AND WIVES

In both France and the United States, although women were excluded from politics, they were valued and even praised as mothers of the republics and nations. In the United States, republican motherhood was cherished. A republic, the founding fathers believed, needed virtuous leaders; therefore, American mothers were expected to rear such moral leaders. In revolutionary France, many philosophers believed that women could not evenly divide their responsibilities as active political citizens and mothers, so many believed that women served a greater civic duty by training future leaders. In both countries, republican wives were valued, too. These wives exhibited unselfish republican duties and sacrificed for the public good as their husbands expended the entrepreneurial spirit necessary to build robust economies. Although women did not gain suffrage at this time in the United States or France, women gained indirect political influence (and power) as republican mothers and wives. They were considered an integral part of a modern-day republic that provided a moral foundation and training for the nation's future leaders.

EARLY DEMANDS FOR SUFFRAGE

Calls for woman suffrage intensified during the early to mid-1800s, but early advocates for

John Stuart Mill was a nineteenth-century English philosopher and writer who championed individualism. He questioned the rules that a patriarchy places on women in his *The Subjection of Women* (1869), and his arguments were used by women's rights advocates.

woman suffrage in France, England, and the United States received little support. In 1848 in France, when Pierre Leroux (1797–1871) called for suffrage for women in local elections, one historian writes, he was "shouted down" by the French legislature.

In England, the call for suffrage began around the same time as the English Reform Bill of 1832, which used the word *person* instead of *male* to describe voters. When English legislator and philosopher John Stuart Mill (1806–1873) and women's associations called for woman suffrage during the mid-1800s, woman suffrage became more of a possibility.

In the antebellum United States, women had gained certain rights, including the right to have custody of children and divorce from an abusive husband. Early women's rights activists included Lucretia Mott (1793–1880) and Elizabeth Cady

Stanton (1815–1902). The pair had met in England during an antislavery conference in June 1840, where they were refused a seat in the assembly and forbidden to speak. The pair vowed to form their own organization to fight against the oppression of women. Eight years later, the pair organized the Seneca Falls Convention in upstate New York. The meeting launched the women's rights movement in earnest and resulted in the Declaration of Sentiments that demanded rights—including suffrage—for women.

Since its beginning, the women's movement included moderates, who believed in incremental change, and radicals, who demanded immediate rights. Radicals in the British suffrage movement used violent tactics during the early 1900s to achieve their objectives. As these suffragists, allied with the labor union movement, were repeatedly jailed, the suffrage movement gained more and more support.

European suffrage efforts were influenced by American events, and vice-versa. The American frontier experience seemed to have an egalitarian influence on American gender, as the hardships of the wilderness and scarcity of men to assume leadership positions had a leveling effect. Another influence on the suffrage movement was the states' rights doctrine, which allowed each state to be sovereign in matters not specifically given by the U.S. Constitution to Congress. One such area was woman suffrage. For instance, women in Wyoming voted in state and local elections in 1869 while women in many other states could not.

American women gained influence and even power in a variety of 1800s reform movements, such as abolition and temperance. These movements addressed similar problems as the women's rights movements and had similar concerns, including eliminating alcohol abuse and alleviating poverty—to name two examples. Women played key roles in such reform movements, but they were still denied voting rights. Vida Scudder and Lillian Wald, for instance, helped start settlement houses in New York.

The National Union of Women's Suffrage Societies, a British women's rights group that avoided violent and riotous tactics, held a march in 1908. The group's slogan was "Law-Abiding—No Party." Pictured below are NUWSS leaders Lady Frances Balfour (1858–1931), Millicent Fawcett (1847–1929), Ethel Snowden (1880–1951), Emily Davies (1830–1921), and Sophie Bryant (1850–1922).

Lucretia Coffin Mott participated in the U.S. women's rights and abolition movements. She worked with Elizabth Cady Stanton in writing the Declaration of Sentiments, an 1848 declaration of women's social and political rights, including suffrage.

THE LOCAL LEVEL

Women often gained voting rights at the local level long before they gained the national vote. Early in the country's history, women did acquire suffrage rights in some states, such as New York, Massachusetts, and New Hampshire. In 1790, New Jersey granted all free inhabitants the right to vote, but the vote was taken away from women in 1807. In Massachusetts, women lost suffrage rights in 1780 yet regained a little in school committee elections in 1879. Voting rights for all local, state, and national elections in Massachusetts were granted with the passage of the Nineteenth Amendment. In Western states, American women were given local and state suffrage rights by the late 1800s, starting with Wyoming in 1869, which became the first state to grant woman suffrage. In Arizona, women were granted suffrage rights from the state's establishment (1912). By 1918, women could vote at the state or local level in 15 states.

Similar trends occurred across the Pacific and Atlantic oceans. In Australia, women voted in local elections by the late 1860s and by 1902, Australian women voted at the national level. In

Europe, European women meanwhile gained suffrage first at the municipal level, too. English women gained the right to vote at the municipal level in 1869 and Scottish women in 1882, yet both could not vote at the national level. Women gained suffrage at the local level in Sweden during the mid-1800s and in Iceland in 1882. Indeed, women's voting rights gained acceptance in the Scandinavian countries before other Western countries. Women voted in Norway starting in 1910, women had political equality in Sweden by 1924, and in Finland women first voted for their representatives in 1906.

In countries influenced heavily by Roman law and the Catholic Church, women gained certain rights and privileges, but still could not vote. By the late 1800s, for example, women served as members of French juries, and in Spain, women served as witnesses for the drawing of wills; however, both could not vote.

ASSERTIVENESS AND SUCCESS

During the 1800s and the first decade of the 1900s, women called for suffrage by emphasizing the maternal role that the ballot gave women in battling social problems. Women's groups at this time included the more militant Women's Social and Political Union (WSPU) of England and the National Women's Party (NWP) of the United States and moderate groups such as the National American Woman Suffrage Association (NAWSA), headed by Susan B. Anthony. The first suffrage amendment was introduced in Congress in 1868. It did not pass.

When World War I started, women demanded suffrage as political equals. To what extent war factors contributed to women's rights is debated among historians, but it is undeniable that the World War I era ushered in change. Throughout the war, women's rights advocates lobbied diligently for national suffrage. Carrie Chapman Catt (1859–1947) led NAWSA efforts at the state level, and the more aggressive NWP unsuccessfully

Elizabeth Cady Stanton (*seated*) and Susan B. Anthony (*standing*) were national leaders in the American women's call for suffrage.

worked in 1916 to defeat Democratic politicians who ignored their calls for national suffrage yet represented the 12 states that had previously granted local and state woman suffrage.

After the 1916 election, NWP and NAWSA activists protested outside the White House and labeled President Woodrow Wilson "Kaiser Wilson," a reference to the autocratic leader of Germany, Kaiser Wilhelm II, because Wilson opposed woman's suffrage. Although the NAWSA leadership expelled the activist members from their organization, the protests undoubtedly affected Wilson's support of the Nineteenth Amendment, for he soon changed his position. The Nineteenth Amendment, based on the Anthony Amendment proposed by suffrage supporters in 1878, was initially ratified by 36 states. In 1920, the amendment became law, and four years after Canada and three years after the Soviet Union had granted woman suffrage, all American women had gained the vote.

Meanwhile, European women had been winning the vote, too, sometimes as a "reward" for their important wartime contributions as nurses, workers in munitions factories, or in other war-related roles. In 1918, Polish, Czech, and Austrian women gained voting rights. That year German women gained political rights, too,

and later in 1919, suffrage. During World War I in Great Britain, the women's rights movement gained more support. In 1918, Parliament granted universal suffrage to all citizens over the age of 30, but this still excluded less than half of the adult women. Ten years later, Parliament in 1928 granted suffrage to all women over 21 years of age.

Other countries acted more slowly. Although French calls for woman's suffrage were among the earliest in the women's rights movement, the nation waited until 1944 to grant women suffrage. Some other European countries, such as Switzerland, granted woman suffrage much later in 1971. Latin American countries typically granted suffrage during the mid-1900s. Asian countries, including India, and African nations such as Liberia, Uganda, and Nigeria, granted woman suffrage in the mid-1900s, too.

Gaining political rights and suffrage did not necessarily mean gaining political advantage. In many places, women still struggled to have a voice in national legislatures and to this day continue to fight for social equality. In many other countries, including Saudi Arabia and United Arab Emirates, however, women still have no political voice.

Troy Kickler

Formed in 1920, the year the Nineteenth Amendment was ratified, the National League of Women's Voters (today known as the League of Women's Voters) worked in the United States at the national, state, and local levels to increase understanding of public policy and to influence public policy decisions. Below is the 1920 board of directors, including Carrie Chapman Catt (*seated far right*), president of the National Woman Suffrage Association (NAWSA) from 1900 to 1904 and 1915 to 1920.

Mrs. Park, President

Mrs. Catt, Honorary President

GUIDED READING

Bridenthal, Renate, and Claudia Koonz, eds. *Becoming Visible: Women in European History.* Boston, MA: Houghton Mifflin, 1977.

Catt, Carrie Chapman, and Nettie Rogers Shulter. *Woman Suffrage and Politics: The Inner Story of the Suffrage Movement.* Buffalo, NY: William S. Hein, 2005.

Clift, Eleanor. *Founding Sisters and the Nineteenth Amendment.* Hoboken, NJ: Wiley, 2003.

Duby, Georges, and Michelle Perrot, eds. *A History of Women in the West.* Cambridge, MA: Belknap, 1994.

Rau, Dana Meachen. *Great Women of the Suffrage Movement.* Minneapolis, MN: Compass Point Books, 2006.

THE STIMSON DOCTRINE AND CHINA

The Stimson Doctrine of 1932 was a U.S. foreign-policy proclamation declaring that the United States would refuse to recognize territorial changes gained through force. The doctrine was issued in response to the 1931 Japanese invasion of the Chinese province of Manchuria. It ushered in an era of growing tensions between the United States and Japan, which culminated in World War II.

Following the acquisition of the Philippines as a result of the Spanish-American War, the United States sought to increase its trade with China. However, the European powers and Japan had carved China into individual spheres of influence, areas that were virtual colonies. The outside powers typically denied access to their spheres of influence to merchants of other countries or levied high customs and duties on imports or exports. In 1899, U.S. Secretary of State John Hay issued a series of diplomatic messages that collectively became known as the Open Door policy. The policy demanded that all merchants be granted the same trade rights and privileges in China. Hay also called on all nations to respect China's territory and sovereignty. He was afraid that the Europeans and Japan would formally colonize China and then shut U.S. merchants out of the market. The Open Door policy remained the cornerstone of America's China policy until the 1920s.

Meanwhile, the 1905 Russo-Japanese War demonstrated the growing military prowess of Japan, which easily defeated Russia. Japan sought to control more of the trade and territory of Asia during a period when the United States was also gaining influence in the region. America sought to maintain open trade, even in areas dominated by Japan and other colonial powers.

POSTWAR INTERNATIONAL RELATIONS

Following World War I, a series of international conferences took place that were designed to maintain world peace through arms control and disarmament. The major combatants of World War I eagerly sought to avoid another global conflict because of the cost in economic terms and the number of deaths resulting from the war.

Between November 1921 and February 1922, representatives from Belgium, China, Great Britain, France, Italy, Japan, the Netherlands, Portugal, and the United States met at the

JOHN HAY (1838–1905)

John Hay was a distinguished American statesman involved in a wide variety of roles inside and outside the political sphere. As a young man, Hay served as an assistant private secretary to Abraham Lincoln. After the Civil War, Hay turned to writing and became a well-known literary figure. His accomplishments in literary circles included a highly touted biography of Lincoln. In 1897, President William McKinley (1843–1901) named Hay ambassador to the United Kingdom. In 1898, Hay became U.S. secretary of state under McKinley and served in the same position for President Theodore Roosevelt. Besides the creation of the Open Door policy with China, Hay was also a central figure in diplomatic efforts to pave the way for the construction of the Panama Canal.

Representing and leading the most important nations in the world at the time, the "Big Nine" stand outside the 1921 World Disarmament Conference in Washington, D.C.

Washington Conference, which aimed to promote disarmament and peace in the Pacific region. The United States sought to fashion a formal agreement to preserve China's sovereignty. The result was the Nine Power Treaty, which affirmed China's territorial integrity—but the treaty did not have any enforcement mechanisms.

On August 27, 1928, as part of the continuing effort to promote world peace, the Kellogg-Briand Pact was signed. The agreement outlawed offensive war. It was created by Frank B. Kellogg (1856–1937), who was U.S. secretary of state at the time, and his French counterpart, Aristide Briand (1862–1932). It was signed by 61 nations, including the United States and Japan. U.S. policymakers believed the agreement would bolster the Nine Power Treaty by eliminating any Japanese threat to China.

JAPANESE AGGRESSION IN MANCHURIA

On September 18, 1931, however, the Japanese military invaded Manchuria. The Japanese sought control of Manchuria's resources, especially the territory's vast agricultural lands and timber deposits. Japan's military correctly predicted that the other nations of the world would not be willing to go to war to defend China. The League of Nations condemned the invasion and called for the invading forces to be withdrawn, but Japan ignored the call and eventually with-

drew from the League in 1933. Meanwhile, fearful of another large-scale war and with the nation's attention focused on the expanding impact of the Great Depression, the United States, led by President Herbert Hoover, also endeavored to use diplomacy to convince Japan to withdraw.

On October 20, Secretary of State Stimson sent identical letters to Japan and China, stating that each nation had obligations to maintain peace. The correspondence had no effect. For the next two months, Stimson attempted to negotiate with Japan. He pressed for economic sanctions against Japan, a policy endorsed by the League of Nations. However, President Hoover felt that sanctions could cause an escalation of the conflict and that the United States could not afford to suspend trade with Japan because of the Depression. Consequently, on November 19, 1931, Stimson informed the League that the United States would not agree to economic sanctions. The League abandoned the idea, since the United States was Japan's largest trading partner and without its participation, economic sanctions would not have a significant impact on Japan.

Declaration of the Stimson Doctrine

Japanese forces took the town of Jinzhou on January 2, 1932, leading to the collapse of the Chinese government in that province. On

January 7, Stimson notified the Japanese and Chinese governments that the United States would not recognize any de facto government or treaty agreements between the two nations that would infringe upon U.S. interests in China. His message to the Japanese government would subsequently be known as the Stimson Doctrine.

Despite Stimson's declaration, the fighting continued and spread to Shanghai, where Japanese marines invaded on January 28, 1932. On February 2, the United States proposed that Japan and China end hostilities through an organized withdrawal of Japanese and Chinese soldiers from Shanghai. The United States also proposed the creation of a neutral commission to settle conflicts between the two nations. China accepted the terms, but Japan's government would not acquiesce.

At first, Great Britain did not support the diplomatic actions of the U.S. government and instead sought to use the League of Nations to mediate the conflict. However, as the hostilities continued to spread, the British decided to present a united front with the Americans. In March, Great Britain presented a resolution to the

Secretary of State Henry L. Stimson shaped American foreign policy in the 1930s.

THE KELLOGG-BRIAND PACT

The Kellogg-Briand Pact, also known as the Pact of Paris, was signed on August 27, 1928, by 15 nations. In the following months, another 60 countries signed the pact renouncing war, which said, in part:

"A frank renunciation of war as an instrument of national policy should be made to the end that the peaceful and friendly relations now existing between their peoples may be perpetuated; Convinced that all changes in their relations with one another should be sought only by pacific means and be the result of a peaceful and orderly process, and that any signatory Power which shall hereafter seek to promote its national interests by resort to war should be denied the benefits furnished by this Treaty; Hopeful that, encouraged by their example, all the other nations of the world will join in this humane endeavor and by adhering to the present Treaty as soon as it comes into force bring their peoples within the scope of its beneficent provisions, thus uniting the civilized nations of the world in a common renunciation of war as an instrument of their national policy."

On January 17, 1929, President Coolidge, with Secretary of State Frank B. Kellogg, Secretary of the Treasury Andrew Mellon, and Secretary of Labor James Davis (*left to right, seated*) signed the Kellogg-Briand Pact. In July, the Pact officially went into effect.

THE ELECTION OF 1932

The conflict in Asia and other foreign policy concerns seemed to go unnoticed among the candidates and voters during the 1932 U.S. presidential election, which focused mainly on domestic issues. With the United States mired in the Great Depression, the campaigns of the Republican candidate, President Hoover, and the Democratic candidate, New York Governor Franklin D. Roosevelt, revolved around the economy. Roosevelt generally agreed with most of Hoover's foreign policy. The Democratic candidate even endorsed the Stimson Doctrine in January 1932 and pledged to continue its nonrecognition policy (which Roosevelt did after he was elected). Roosevelt won the election because of discontent with Hoover's economic policy, rather than his foreign policy.

League that incorporated, verbatim, the Stimson Doctrine. On March 11, 1932, the resolution was adopted by the League.

THE LYTTON COMMISSION

As the Manchuria crisis continued, the League of Nations set up the Lytton Commission, led by British politician Victor Bulwer-Lytton (1876–1947), to investigate Japanese actions in Manchuria. The commission reported that Japan had invaded the region and created a government in the province against citizens' wishes. The overall Japanese military campaign was viewed as inconsistent with international law. The League assembly adopted the report on February 24, 1933. The Japanese delegation was outraged, and walked out of the assembly. Soon after, Japan withdrew from the League of Nations.

Throughout the 1930s, the United States continued to follow the Stimson Doctrine of nonrecognition. However, this policy did not stop Japan's aggression toward China. As Japan became an even greater military power, its imperialistic attitude increased. In 1937, Japan invaded the Chinese city of Peking (now Beijing) in a new Sino-Japanese war. By the time the Chinese port city of Guangzhou fell in 1938, Japanese forces on the Chinese mainland totaled nearly 1 million. The Stimson Doctrine failed to stop further Japanese aggression, but it continued to be a major component of U.S. foreign policy. After World War II, when the Soviet Union occupied Estonia, Latvia, and Lithuania, the United States invoked the Stimson Doctrine and refused to recognize the Soviet annexation of the three Baltic countries.

Gavin Wilk

The Lytton Commission published its report on the Manchurian Question in October 1932, for the League of Nations.

GUIDED READING

Hodgson, Godfrey. *The Colonel: The Life and Wars of Henry Stimson, 1867–1950.* New York: Knopf, 1990.

Langer, Robert. *Seizure of Territory: The Stimson Doctrine and Related Principles in Legal Theory and Diplomatic Practice.* New York: Greenwood Press, 1969.

Schmitz, David F. *Henry Stimson: The First Wise Man.* Wilmington, DE: Scholarly Resources, 2001.

Vitas, Robert A. *The United States and Lithuania: The Stimson Doctrine of Nonrecognition.* New York: Praeger, 1990.

WORLD WAR II

World War II (1939–1945) was the largest and most costly conflict in human history. The war pitted the Allies—including China, Great Britain, France, and the United States—against the Axis Powers, led by Germany, Italy, and Japan. World War II dramatically altered global politics and left the United States and the Soviet Union as the world's two remaining superpowers.

The Treaty of Versailles (1919), which ended World War I, redrew the political boundaries of Europe. Even before the end of the war, communism, a political and economic system in which there is no private ownership of property, emerged in Russia, which changed its name to the Union of Soviet Socialist Republics. Meanwhile, fascism, a political ideology based on authoritarianism, extreme militarism, and expansionism, came to dominate Italy, Germany, and Japan.

ROAD TO WAR

By the early 1930s, a range of challenges had arisen in the post–World War I international order. Both Japan and Italy had launched aggressive wars to conquer new territory, with Japan invading Manchuria in 1931 and Italy attacking Ethiopia in 1935. In Germany, Adolf Hitler, the head of the fascist Nazi Party, became leader of the country in 1933. Hitler repudiated the main tenets of the Treaty of Versailles and began to rebuild Germany's military.

During the late 1930s, Germany embarked on an effort to expand its territory. In 1936, German troops reoccupied the Rhineland, which had been placed under French control at the end of World War I. Germany forced a union with Austria in March 1938, and invaded Czechoslovakia in September. Hitler also sought to annex the Sudetenland, an area with a large ethnic German population. The invasion provoked an international crisis, and world leaders met at the Munich Conference in 1938 to negotiate a response. Led by British Prime Minister Neville Chamberlain (1869–1940), the leaders agreed on a policy of appeasement, whereby Germany's demands were granted in exchange for the avoidance of a major war. Appeasement

emboldened Hitler, who now believed that Britain and France would not go to war to stop German territorial expansion. In March 1939, Hitler invaded and conquered the rest of Czechoslovakia.

Hitler initiated a brutal, dictatorial regime in Germany, whereby those who opposed his regime were persecuted. Hitler and the Nazis particularly targeted Jews and embraced a virulent form of anti-Semitism. Beginning with the 1935 Nuremburg Laws, a succession of measures were enacted took away the right and civil liberties of Jews, including prohibitions on marriage between Jews and non-Jews and the eventual loss of citizenship for people of Jewish heritage. Political opponents of Hitler's regime, criminals, Jews, and other people labeled as "undesirable" by the Nazis were sent to concentration camps, a series of brutal penal facilities.

In 1939, Hitler, one of the most vehement anti-communist figures in the world, stunned other leaders when Germany and the Soviet Union announced a nonaggression pact. Through it, Hitler sought to ensure that the Soviets would not oppose a planned invasion of Poland. This would allow Germany to avoid the mistakes of World War I, when it had to fight a war on two fronts. The pact had a secret clause in which Poland was divided between Germany and the Soviet Union, and Moscow was allowed control over the Balkan nations of Estonia, Latvia, and Lithuania. Concurrently, freed from the threat of a conflict with Germany, the Soviets planned an invasion of Finland.

WAR IN EUROPE

On September 1, 1939, German forces attacked Poland. Based on his experiences with Czechoslovakia, Hitler believed that the Western Allies would not go to war, but he miscalculated. Two days later, Great Britain and France declared war against Germany. Within a week, the states of the British Commonwealth, including Australia, Canada, and New Zealand, also declared war. The Allies were unable to deploy significant numbers of troops to Poland, which was overrun by the Germans within five weeks. Germany employed a new style of warfare that combined aerial assaults and quick armored thrusts. Known as *blitzkrieg* or "lightning war," the new tactic quickly overwhelmed Poland, which also faced a Soviet invasion on September 17.

By early October, Poland had fallen to the German Army. Here, on October 10, 1939, German cavalry pass through the war-torn streets of Warsaw, publicly displaying the German war machine.

With the fall of Poland, the focus of the war shifted to the west. Throughout 1939, British and Commonwealth troops went to France, where the war was marked by a series of skirmishes along the German-French border. In April 1940, Germany invaded Denmark and Norway, quickly overwhelming both countries.

In May 1940, British Prime Minister Chamberlain, whose appeasement policy had allowed Hitler to dominate the European continent, resigned, and Winston Churchill became Britain's new leader. On May 10, the same day that Churchill became prime minister, the German military smashed into Holland, Luxembourg, and Belgium, using its blitzkrieg tactics to overrun the countries. German forces were now able to invade France from the north. The Allied army became encircled and had to evacuate at Dunkirk. Although a defeat, the retreat saved the core of the British army for future combat. By June 4, some 200,000 British troops had been rescued, along with almost 140,000 French soldiers. On June 10, Italy declared war on Britain and France. On June 14, Paris fell to the Germans. France surrendered to

Germany on June 22. The Germans had accomplished in a year what they had not been able to achieve in four years of fighting during World War I.

GLOBAL WAR

On September 27, 1940, Germany, Italy, and Japan solidified their prewar alliance with the Tripartite Pact. Italy, having attacked British colonies in Africa in August 1940, intended to take additional territory in Africa as well as conquer and share the European continent with Germany, while Japan sought domination in Asia and the Pacific. Hungary and Romania later joined the Axis Powers. In October 1940, Italy launched an invasion of Greece. The Allies stopped the Italians in Greece, forcing Germany to divert men and materials to aid their ally. British and Commonwealth forces also successfully held their ground against the Italians in North Africa, and the Germans were forced to deploy troops there as well. In April 1941, both Greece and Yugoslavia fell to combined German-Italian forces, but fighting continued in North Africa.

War in Europe

The fall of France left Britain as the sole European Allied Power fighting against the Axis. German military leaders attempted to force Britain into surrender through a combination of bombing and naval attacks, in what became known as the Battle of Britain. The aerial bombardment was designed to destroy Britain's military facilities and its industrial capacity while undermining its morale. The naval campaign, which used submarines and surface ships to attack merchant convoys, was meant to cut off supplies to the British Isles. Britain's Royal Air Force (RAF) conducted a desperate but effective campaign against the German air force, or Luftwaffe.

The United States remained officially neutral, but it came to Great Britain's assistance in September 1940 by reinforcing the British naval fleet with 50 World War I–era destroyers in exchange for U.S. rights to use military bases in Canada and the Caribbean. In the spring of 1941, American aid was increased after the passing of the Lend-Lease Act, which supplied Great Britain with vast amounts of war supplies in return for more military bases.

Hitler, unable to conquer Britain, turned the focus of the German military to the east. On June 22, 1941, Germany effectively nullified its prewar alliance with the Soviet Union and launched Operation Barbarossa, a massive, surprise invasion against the Soviet Union. German armor and infantry quickly overran Soviet positions and advanced deep into the Soviet Union. Shocked by the invasion, Soviet leader Josef Stalin turned to the Allies for support. On July 12, the British agreed to provide badly needed military supplies to the Soviets.

Pearl Harbor

The United States imposed oil and steel sanctions on Japan in 1941 in response to Japan's continuing war with China (the Second Sino-Japanese War, 1937–1945). Other nations, including Britain and the Netherlands' East India colonies, followed suit. In addition, America provided military assistance to China, including funding the deployment of three fighter squadrons known as the Flying Tigers. The loss of precious resources constrained Japan's ability to continue its campaigns in China, and U.S. support for the Chinese military angered Japanese military officials. As a result, Japan decided to launch a surprise attack on the United States.

On the morning of December 7, 1941, the Japanese military struck Pearl Harbor, destroying most of the U.S. battleships in the Pacific, but missing the important aircraft carrier fleet that was away on maneuvers. The attack killed 2,402 military personnel and civilians and was the deadliest strike to take place on U.S. soil until the terrorist attacks of September 11, 2001. The United States and Great Britain declared war on Japan on December 8. Three days later, Germany and Italy declared war on the United States. During the Arcadia Conference in Washington, D.C., which began on December 22, 1941, the Allies agreed on a "Europe First" strategy. They would concentrate their resources on winning the war in Europe before transferring assets to the Pacific, and to their fight against Germany and the rest of the Axis Powers.

On December 8, Japan attacked the Philippines, a U.S. territory in the South Pacific. Japan subsequently conquered most of the American Pacific territories, including Guam and Wake Island, and a range of British, French, and Dutch colonies. By summer 1942, the Japanese empire was at its height and stretched from Manchuria in the north to New Guinea in the south.

Even prior to the attack on Pearl Harbor, the United States was in the midst of a dramatic economic expansion as the nation was transitioning to a war economy. The government had ordered massive amounts of military supplies, both to arm the growing American military and to supply the Allies. U.S. gross domestic product increased from $800 billion in 1938 to $1.1 trillion in 1941 and $2.34 trillion in 1945. Meanwhile, in September 1940, Congress enacted conscription, and the nation began building its military. The U.S. Army numbered just 174,000 in 1939, but ballooned to 1.67 million by the time of Japan's attack on Pearl Harbor and reached 8.3 million by 1945. America's entry into the war would make a dramatic difference to the Allies because of its industrial and human resources.

The USS *Maryland* stood firm throughout the Japanese bombing of Pearl Harbor. Although slightly damaged, the battleship was able to quickly rejoin the American fleet after the attack.

THE "DAY OF INFAMY" SPEECH

On December 8, 1941, one day after Japan's deadly assault on Pearl Harbor, President Roosevelt delivered a dramatic message to Congress asking for a declaration of war. In his speech, he called December 7, 1941, a date that would "live in infamy." He said, in part:

"No matter how long it may take us to overcome this premeditated invasion, the American people in their righteous might will win through to absolute victory.

I believe that I interpret the will of the Congress and of the people when I assert that we will not only defend ourselves to the uttermost, but will make it very certain that this form of treachery shall never again endanger us. ... I ask that the Congress declare that since the unprovoked and dastardly attack by Japan on Sunday, December 7, 1941, a state of war has existed between the United States and the Japanese empire."

THE TIDE OF WAR TURNS

In December 1941, the Soviets stopped the Germans less than 20 miles (32 kilometers) from Moscow. The Germans had expected a rapid advance and quick victory and were not prepared for a long, drawn-out campaign. A particularly harsh winter further complicated the German offensive. The Soviets launched a massive counteroffensive after the Germans failed to conquer Moscow, but the Germans fought the Soviets to a stalemate.

The fighting in the Soviet Union was brutal. Both sides committed atrocities, and large numbers of civilians were killed (an estimated 14 to 17 million). Most were killed by the Nazis and other Axis forces, but others were killed by Soviet forces or died of disease or starvation. Many deaths were caused by the "scorched-earth policy" adopted by Stalin, whereby any resources or goods that might have been useful to the invaders were destroyed by retreating Soviet forces. The Battle of Stalingrad, which began in July 1942 and lasted until February 1943, was the turning point in the war on the eastern front. About 850,000 Axis forces were killed, wounded, or captured, while the Soviets suffered more than 1.1 million casualties. The superior numbers of the Soviet forces wore down the Germans and resulted in a badly needed Allied victory.

Meanwhile, by 1942, British and British Commonwealth forces had fought the combined German and Italian forces to a stalemate in northern Africa. On November 8, 1942, American General Dwight D. Eisenhower (1890–1969) led Operation Torch, the first Anglo-American offensive in World War II. The amphibious action took place along the North African coast from Safi to Algiers. It consisted of more than 107,000 Allied troops and more than 600 ships. The invasion caught the Axis forces by surprise and led to their rapid retreat. By spring 1943, Allied forces had overtaken the Axis forces and gained control of North Africa.

In January 1943, Roosevelt and Churchill had secretly met in northern Africa in Casablanca, Morocco, for their first wartime conference. The two leaders discussed the future invasion of Italy and agreed to demand an unconditional surrender of the Axis countries.

In July 1943, the Allies conquered Sicily. The Italian dictator, Benito Mussolini (1883–1945)

was overthrown by Italian military and civilian leaders who believed the Axis Powers were losing the war. The new Italian government launched peace negotiations with the Allies and signed an armistice on September 9. Allied forces entered the Italian mainland in September, and the new Italian government declared war on Germany that same month. German troops were rushed into northern and central Italy, slowing the Allied advance.

Across the Pacific, the U.S. Navy had begun a series of effective naval actions against Japan, starting with the Battle of Midway from June 4 to June 7, 1942. The battle secured the American naval base at Midway and ended the overall Japanese Pacific offensive. The U.S. Navy, which had been decimated in Pearl Harbor 18 months earlier, now proved its superiority over Japan. The Allied strategy in the Pacific became characterized by "island-hopping"—taking or retaking Japanese-held islands, one by one, as the Allies inched closer to the Japanese home islands.

D-DAY

On June 6, 1944, Allied forces under the command of Eisenhower launched a long-awaited invasion of France. More than 150,000 Allied soldiers stormed the French coast at Normandy or were parachuted into the countryside. Once

D-Day was one of the greatest military operations in the history of warfare. Here, troops of the 2nd Infantry Division march up from the beaches on June 8, 1944, one day after landing in France.

in control of the coast, the Allies poured men and material into northern France to drive the Germans deeper into the French countryside, as they retreated back toward Germany. Paris was liberated on August 24, 1944. By the end of September, the Allies were in Germany.

The German army launched one last desperate attack on Allied forces in late 1944. For six weeks until the end of January 1945, the Battle of the Bulge raged in dire weather conditions and resulted in 180,000 American and German casualties. Once the Allies regrouped and thwarted the Germans, it was clear that the war in Europe would soon be over, and Allied leaders planned for victory.

THE WAR ENDS

Two months after attending the Yalta Conference, a planning meeting for the postwar world, President Roosevelt died, leaving Vice President Harry S Truman (1884–1972) as the new president. At the time of Roosevelt's death, American and British forces were gathering momentum in Germany, and on April 25, Soviet troops linked up with American forces that had crossed the River Elbe to the west of Berlin. Hitler committed suicide on April 30 in an underground bunker while Soviet forces took control of Berlin. On May 7, 1945, Germany officially surrendered to the Allies. As the Allies took control of German-occupied territory, the true extent of the atrocities of the Nazi regime became apparent. The Nazis had created a series of death and labor camps where some 9 to 11 million people, including more than 6 million Jews, were murdered, in what came to be known as the Holocaust.

With Germany defeated, the Allies concentrated on defeating Japan. More islands were retaken in the Pacific, including Guam and the Philippines. In addition, the United States initiated bombing raids on Japan. In February 1945, the strategically important island of Iwo Jima was invaded. In June 1945, the island of Okinawa was captured by American forces. Japan was now only 300 miles (480 kilometers) away.

The United States dropped a new weapon—the atomic bomb—on the Japanese city of Hiroshima on August 6, 1945. On August 9, the same day that the Soviet Union attacked Japanese-held Manchuria, another atomic bomb was dropped on Nagasaki. Japan, faced with the carnage created by the new superweapon, surrendered to the Allies.

World War II left between 50 and 70 million soldiers and civilians dead. More than 20 million Soviets and 20 million Chinese died. About 7.2 million Germans, 5.6 million Poles, and 2.7 million Japanese died. The war left more than a million dead from Yugoslavia, while Italy had 454,500 dead and Great Britain had 449,800 dead, and the United States had 418,500 dead. The United States emerged as the global leader of the postwar world. The American economy that helped to win the war for the Allies assisted in the redevelopment of Europe and Japan. The American war arsenal—which now included the atomic bomb—propelled the American military to the pinnacle of international dominance, a position that would soon be challenged by the ensuing cold war.

Gavin Wilk

GUIDED READING

Ambrose, Stephen E. *Citizen Soldiers: The U.S. Army from the Normandy Beaches to the Bulge to the Surrender of Germany.* New York: Simon & Schuster, 1998.

Ambrose, Stephen E. *The Victors: Eisenhower and His Boys: The Men of World War II.* New York: Simon & Schuster, 1998.

Dunnigan, James F., and Albert A. Nofi. *Victory at Sea: World War II in the Pacific.* New York: William Morrow, 1995.

Gilbert, Martin. *The Second World War: A Complete History.* New York: Henry Holt, 1989.

Shirer, William L. *The Rise and Fall of the Third Reich: A History of Nazi Germany.* New York: Simon & Schuster, 1960.

ARMED NEUTRALITY AND LEND LEASE

Armed neutrality was the U.S. policy toward the belligerent nations involved in World War II before America joined the conflict. The administration of President Franklin D. Roosevelt warned that the nation would use military force against any country that violated the rights of the United States. However, the United States also enacted a number of programs to assist the nations fighting the Axis Powers, including the Lend-Lease Act through which American military equipment was "lent" to the Allies in exchange for allowing the United States to "lease" military bases.

On September 5, 1939, four days after the outbreak of fighting in Europe, President Roosevelt declared that the United States would remain neutral. At the same time, he began preparations to secure the nation's interests. The United States, where isolationism remained strong, still adhered to the Neutrality Act of 1935, which outlawed the exportation of arms to warring nations. In addition, restrictions were put in place in 1937 that made it illegal for American ships and citizens to travel into war zones.

NEUTRALITY AND NATIONAL SECURITY

Two weeks after the war began, Roosevelt addressed Congress and urged repeal of certain parts of the Neutrality Act. The president spoke of the tumultuous events in Europe and the need for steps to secure the United States. Roosevelt's speech offered reassurance that the United States would not be brought into the European conflict, while at the same time requesting that the arms embargo stipulated in the Neutrality Act be lifted. The president believed that providing arms to nations defending themselves against Germany would make it unnecessary for the United States to place troops on foreign soil and was in the best interests of national security.

In early October 1939, representatives of 21 American republics signed the Declaration of Panama, which declared that the waters 300 miles (480 kilometers) off the coast of North and South America would be considered neutrality zones. The U.S. Navy, which weeks before had begun defensive preparations for possible attack, began to send naval patrols to positions along the East Coast, from the Caribbean Islands to the waters off the coast of Maine. These patrols prohibited ships of warring nations from coming close to shore.

PUBLIC NEUTRALITY, PRIVATE SUPPORT

As the question of U.S. neutrality was debated in Congress, German forces quickly swept through Europe, overtaking Poland and threatening France. Two months after the start of fighting, on November 4, 1939, Congress passed an amended neutrality act. The Neutrality Act of 1939 allowed the United States to sell arms on a cash-and-carry basis.

In 1940, while continuing to state the importance of American neutrality in public

In September 1939, President Franklin D. Roosevelt appealed to Congress to lift certain parts of the Neutrality Act in order to give the United States greater flexibility in its foreign relations.

pronouncements, President Roosevelt privately recognized that U.S. participation was likely unavoidable. On May 19, 1940, Winston Churchill became prime minister of Great Britain and immediately called for greater American assistance. Roosevelt, faced with a presidential election in November, attempted to publicly appease the isolationist forces in the United States, while quietly initiating plans to supply Britain with war materials.

By June 1940, German troops had entered the streets of Paris, and German U-boats (submarines) attacked British shipping. The English Channel was all that separated Great Britain from German invasion. In that context, the United States and Great Britain brokered a deal whereby 50 World War I–era American destroyers were sent to Britain and Canada in return for 99-year leases to British territory in Canada and the Caribbean that would be used as U.S. naval and air bases. The program was known as the Destroyers for Bases initiative, and it became the basis for the Lend-Lease program. Roosevelt bypassed the cash requirements of the Neutrality Act by arguing that the cash value of the leases equaled the value of the equipment transferred to the Allies.

THE "ARSENAL OF DEMOCRACY"

After his reelection to an unprecedented third term in 1940, Roosevelt began considering other options that would arm the Allies against Germany and its Axis partners, Italy and Japan. During this period, the British people were subjected to daily bombings by the German Luftwaffe (air force). Faced with crippling production costs and the possibility of a German invasion, Churchill requested major shipments of U.S. war materiel.

Roosevelt began speaking publicly of the necessity to assist Great Britain and other Allies in order to alleviate the threat of German aggression. The United States, he declared, should be an "arsenal of democracy." For the next two months, members of Congress debated Roosevelt's call for greater action, and on March 11, 1941, passed the Lend-Lease Act. Under the measure, the United States was authorized to send unlimited weapons, ships, tanks, and aircraft to Britain and other nations fighting the Axis countries. It also expanded the Destroyers for Bases program.

In August 1941, President Roosevelt and British Prime Minister Churchill held a secret meeting aboard a U.S. destroyer off the coast of Newfoundland, Canada, referred to as the Atlantic Conference. The purpose of the meeting was to discuss war preparations and prospects for the postwar world. To Churchill's dismay, however, Roosevelt continued to insist on American neutrality. On August 14, the two leaders signed the Atlantic Charter, which proclaimed their mutual belief in self-determination and the destruction of Nazi Germany.

At the time of the Atlantic Conference, German forces had infiltrated deep into Soviet territory. W. Averell Harriman (1891–1986), the U.S. Lend-Lease representative to Britain, was soon sent to Moscow to discuss supplying the Soviets with weapons. Harriman and a British representative met with Soviet officials and discussed further lend-lease arrangements. Under the Moscow Protocol, signed on October 1, the United States opened the American arsenal to the Soviet Union as well, and the Lend-Lease program was also extended to China and other Allied countries. By the end of the war, through the Lend-Lease program, the United States sent more than $50 billion in weapons and supplies to the Allies. The majority, valued at approximately $31.4 billion, went to Great Britain, followed by the Soviet Union, which received approximately $11.3 billion.

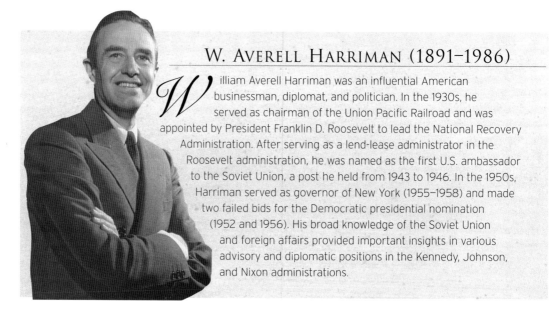

W. AVERELL HARRIMAN (1891–1986)

William Averell Harriman was an influential American businessman, diplomat, and politician. In the 1930s, he served as chairman of the Union Pacific Railroad and was appointed by President Franklin D. Roosevelt to lead the National Recovery Administration. After serving as a lend-lease administrator in the Roosevelt administration, he was named as the first U.S. ambassador to the Soviet Union, a post he held from 1943 to 1946. In the 1950s, Harriman served as governor of New York (1955–1958) and made two failed bids for the Democratic presidential nomination (1952 and 1956). His broad knowledge of the Soviet Union and foreign affairs provided important insights in various advisory and diplomatic positions in the Kennedy, Johnson, and Nixon administrations.

The Atlantic Conference of 1941 allowed President Roosevelt to meet and discuss future American-British relations with British Prime Minister Winston Churchill. Here, the two leaders sat and talked while waiting for a church service to begin during the conference.

THE END OF NEUTRALITY

On September 11, 1941, President Roosevelt announced that U.S. warships would defend themselves against German or any other Axis vessels that ventured into American waters. The announcement came following a number of German attacks on a succession of American ships. Meanwhile, the U.S. Navy also began secretly to escort British convoys. From September to November 1941, the United States continued to take defensive measures against the German navy.

American neutrality came to an abrupt end after the Japanese attack on Pearl Harbor on December 7, 1941. The next day, after President Roosevelt's historic address to Congress, the United States officially declared war on Japan—which responded in kind. On December 11, Germany and Italy declared war on the United States—and the United States declared war on the European Axis. By January 1942, American ships filled with American war supplies—and American troops—began arriving in Europe.

Gavin Wilk

GUIDED READING

Black, Conrad. *Franklin Delano Roosevelt: Champion of Freedom.* New York: Weidenfeld & Nicolson, 2003.

Davis, Kenneth S. *FDR: Into the Storm 1937–1940.* New York: Random House, 1993.

Franklin D. Roosevelt Presidential Library and Museum. http://www.fdrlibrary.marist.edu.

Kershaw, Ian. *Fateful Choices: Ten Decisions That Changed The World, 1940–1941.* New York: Penguin Press, 2007.

Kimball, Warren E. *Forged In War: Roosevelt, Churchill, and the Second World War.* New York: William Morrow, 1997.

Hiroshima and Nagasaki

On August 6, 1945, the Enola Gay, a U.S. B-29 Superfortress bomber, dropped an atomic bomb on the city of Hiroshima, Japan. A total of 70,000 residents died immediately, and another 130,000 perished subsequently as a result of injuries or radiation poisoning. Three days later, on August 9, another B-29 dropped a second atomic bomb on Nagasaki, killing 70,000. The two attacks forced a Japanese surrender and brought World War II to an end.

The birth of the atomic bomb can be traced to prewar Germany, where, on December 9, 1938, German scientists Otto Hahn (1879–1968) and Fritz Strassman (1902–1980) succeeded for the first time in splitting an atom. Four months later, physicist Leo Szilard (1898–1964), a Hungarian Jew who had fled Germany in 1933 and came to the United States five years later, created a chain reaction of uranium in a laboratory. He believed that a nuclear chain reaction could serve as the basis for a new weapon, the atomic bomb.

THE MANHATTAN PROJECT

In 1942, after further studies and nuclear fission testing, the U.S. government initiated a secret program called the Manhattan Project, a dual effort led by the Office of Scientific Research and Development and the U.S. Army Corps of Engineers. Directed by scientist J. Robert Oppenheimer (1904–1967), Manhattan Project scientists worked feverishly for the next three years to create the world's first atomic weapon. On July 16, 1945, the atomic bomb was successfully tested in the desert of New Mexico. The mile (1.6-kilometer) radius around the bomb site was annihilated. All plant and animal life ceased to exist.

POTSDAM CONFERENCE

U.S. President Harry Truman, British Prime Minister Winston Churchill, and Soviet Premier Joseph Stalin began a series of meetings on July 17 in Potsdam, a suburb of Berlin, to discuss postwar Europe and the Allied strategy in Japan. On that same day, Allied bombers taking off from American and British aircraft carriers

A Letter to the President

In August 1939, Leo Szilard and Albert Einstein (1879–1955), Jewish émigrés who had fled Nazi Germany, wrote a letter to President Franklin D. Roosevelt. It described developments in nuclear energy and warned the president that Germany might be working on such a weapon. The letter helped convince Roosevelt to initiate the Manhattan Project:

"In the course of the last four months it has been made probable—through the work of Joliot in France as well as Fermi and Szilard in America—that it may become possible to set up a nuclear chain reaction in a large mass of uranium, by which vast amounts of power and large quantities of new radium-like elements would be generated. Now it appears almost certain that this could be achieved in the immediate future.

This new phenomenon would also lead to the construction of bombs, and it is conceivable—though much less certain—that extremely powerful bombs of a new type may thus be constructed. A single bomb of this type, carried by boat and exploded in a port, might very well destroy the whole port together with some of the surrounding territory. However, such bombs might very well prove to be too heavy for transportation by air."

J. ROBERT OPPENHEIMER (1904–1967)

J. Robert Oppenheimer, the "father of the atomic bomb," was one of the most respected American scientists in the twentieth century. He first came into national prominence with his work on theoretical physics. In 1942, General Leslie Groves appointed Oppenheimer scientific director of the Manhattan Project. Oppenheimer led a team of 3,000 people at top-secret laboratories in Los Alamos, New Mexico, and under his guidance, the atomic bomb was created. After World War II, Oppenheimer was appointed chairman of the General Advisory Committee to the Atomic Energy Commission. However, he became concerned over the growing nuclear arms race with the Soviet Union. Oppenheimer opposed the creation of the hydrogen bomb. He was investigated during the McCarthy period and had his security clearance revoked in 1953 because of his past association with Communists in the United States. Oppenheimer retired from public life, but remained critical of the U.S. arms program.

Leslie R. Groves (*left*) appointed J. Robert Oppenheimer (*right*) head of the Los Alamos laboratories.

successfully bombed Japanese industrial towns, military installations, and airfields—but Japan still would not surrender.

During the Potsdam Conference, American Secretary of War Henry Stimson gave British Prime Minister Churchill details of the atomic bomb testing. American and British leaders realized that an invasion of Japan by Allied forces would result in countless casualties and that the atomic bomb could mitigate such loses. On July 26, 1945, the United States, Great Britain, and China delivered a declaration to Japan, stating the necessity for complete and unconditional surrender. After the Allied conditions of the proposed surrender were set, Truman mentioned to Stalin that the United States was in possession of a weapon that could create major destruction. Stalin took the news casually. He had in fact already been made aware of the atomic bomb research by Soviet intelligence sources.

The Bombing of Hiroshima

As the Potsdam Declaration was delivered to Japan, the American cruiser, USS *Indianapolis* arrived on Tinian Island in the western Pacific, carrying the atomic bomb. Having received the terms of the Potsdam Declaration, Japanese Prime Minister Admiral Kantaro Suzuki (1868–1948) publicly rejected the treaty due to its call for an unconditional surrender.

Faced with Japan's rejection, the *Enola Gay* was soon fitted with the atomic bomb, and on August 5, it took off for the 1,700-mile (2,700-kilometer) journey from Tinian Island to its target destination. The *Enola Gay* dropped the atomic bomb on Hiroshima, which completely destroyed about 4.4 square miles (11.4 square kilometers) of the city.

INVASION OF MANCHURIA AND THE BOMBING AT NAGASAKI

On August 8, 1945, the Soviet Union declared war on Japan. The Soviets invaded Japanese-controlled Manchuria the next day, which placed further pressure on Japan to surrender to the Allies. As the Soviets rushed into Manchuria, the United States dropped a second atomic bomb on Nagasaki. After the Hiroshima bombing, Emperor Hirohito of Japan (1901–1989), immediately advised the Japanese Supreme Council for the Direction of the War that Japan must surrender. But an extremist faction of the

council expressed a desire to continue the war. However, after the Nagasaki bomb was dropped, Emperor Hirohito took control and issued an imperial rescript, which declared the end of the war.

JAPANESE SURRENDER

On August 10, the Japanese government offered to surrender, but not unconditionally. The Japanese sought to retain their emperor as head of state. Initially skeptical of the condition, Truman and his administration decided the emperor could remain in place, but his power would be controlled by the Allied supreme commander.

On August 14, Japan announced that it would surrender. The atomic bombs may have saved the Allies from having to invade Japan, but the bombs brought horrific death and devastation to the citizens of Hiroshima and Nagasaki. The threat of nuclear weapons came to dominate the postwar world. The nuclear monopoly of the United States was broken in 1949 when the Soviet Union tested its first atomic weapon. Through the cold war, the superpower conflict revolved around a succession of nuclear arms races where both the United States and the Soviet Union sought to develop and stockpile larger and more powerful weapons.

Gavin Wilk

GUIDED READING

Takaki, Ronald. *Hiroshima: Why America Dropped the Atomic Bomb*. New York: Little, Brown, 1995.

Walker, Stephen. *Shockwave: Countdown to Hiroshima*. New York: HarperCollins, 2005.

Weintraub, Stanley. *The Last Great Victory: The End of World War II, July/August 1945*. New York: Truman Talley Books/Dutton, 1995.

In August 1946, Hiroshima was completely destroyed by an atomic bomb.

THE UNITED NATIONS AND NEW WORLD ORDER

The United Nations (UN) was created in the aftermath of World War II to promote international peace and stability by preventing another global conflict. Designed to avoid the mistakes of its predecessor, the League of Nations, the UN nonetheless struggled to define its role and authority in the cold-war era.

The concept of the United Nations was first proposed at the Dumbarton Oaks Conference in 1944 and then formalized at the San Francisco Conference in 1945 by representatives of the major Allied Powers of World War II, including the United States, the Soviet Union, China, Great Britain, France, and 45 other nations. Representatives drafted the UN Charter. The founding document created a Security Council of 15 member nations, led by five permanent members—the United States, the Soviet Union (later the Russian Federation), the Republic of China (later the People's Republic of China),

France, and the United Kingdom. These five members are the only nations that may veto resolutions before the Security Council. The council is the only UN body that can make binding resolutions. All nations of the world may participate in the General Assembly, the main deliberative body of the UN, and in the other agencies and bureaus of the world body. The UN was officially established on October 24, 1945, following ratification of the organization's charter by the five permanent members of the Security Council and a majority of the other 46 signatories of the UN Charter.

The United Nations was officially created in June 1945 within the confines of the San Francisco Opera House.

PREAMBLE OF THE UN CHARTER

The UN Charter, recognized as the organization's governing treaty, was signed on June 26, 1945, by the 50 countries at the San Francisco Conference. (Poland would sign the charter on October 15 after the formulation of its new government.) The UN charter begins:

"We the peoples of the United Nations determined to save succeeding generations from the scourge of war, which twice in our lifetime has brought untold sorrow to mankind, and to reaffirm faith in fundamental human rights, in the dignity and worth of the human person, in the equal rights of men and women and of nations large and small, and to establish conditions under which justice and respect for the obligations arising from treaties and other sources of international law can be maintained, and to promote social progress and better standards of life in larger freedom, and for these ends to practice tolerance and live together in peace with one another as good neighbors, and to unite our strength to maintain international peace and security, and to ensure, by the acceptance of principles and the institution of methods, that armed force shall not be used, save in the common interest, and to employ international machinery for the promotion of the economic and social advancement of all peoples, have resolved to combine our efforts to accomplish these aims accordingly, our respective Governments, through representatives assembled in the city of San Francisco, who have exhibited their full powers found to be in good and due form, have agreed to the present Charter of the United Nations and do hereby establish an international organization to be known as the United Nations."

EARLY YEARS

The newly formed UN was asked to mediate a number of disputes. For instance, in January 1946, the Security Council initiated discussions over the continued presence of Soviet troops in Northern Iran and helped mediate the withdrawal of the troops over the next year. The UN also managed a number of crises linked to decolonization. In 1947, for example, the UN developed a plan to transition the territory of Palestine to independence. The UN plan included both a Jewish and a Palestinian state; however, on May 14, 1948, one day before the British relinquished control, Jewish independence groups declared the state of Israel and seized formal control of the region. The United States recognized Israel the following day.

A coalition of Arab nations immediately attacked Israel. The UN dispatched Swedish representative Count Folke Bernadotte (1895–1948) and American representative Ralph Bunche (1904–1971) to mediate the conflict. Count Bernadotte, who led the negotiations, was assassinated on September 17, 1948, by Jewish radicals who were against the proposed peace terms. This marked the first act of violence ever against a UN representative. However, Bunche persevered in the mediations, and an armistice was signed on February 24, 1949, although a lasting peace remained elusive. The UN continues to undertake peace efforts in the region.

Korea

The next major test of the UN occurred when Communist North Korea invaded South Korea in June 1950. At the time, the Soviet representative was boycotting Security Council meetings in protest over the refusal of the pro-U.S. members of the world body to allow the representatives of the Communist People's Republic of China (PRC) to assume China's place at the UN instead of representatives of the Nationalist government which had been overthrown in 1949 and forced into exile in Taiwan. With the Soviets absent, the United States secured a resolution that called on all UN members to assist South Korea in fighting the North. The United States led a coalition of UN states against North Korea and the PRC during the Korean War. By 1952, the fighting had stalemated and was ended with an armistice the following year. The

UN continued to participate in efforts to permanently end the Korean conflict and later resolve the North Korean nuclear crisis of the 1990s.

The Suez Crisis

After Egyptian President Gamal Abdel Nasser (1918–1970) nationalized the Suez Canal in 1956, British, French, and Israeli troops secured the waterway. The United States opposed the military venture because of concerns that the intervention would turn the Arab states against the U.S. and its allies. The administration of Dwight D. Eisenhower (1890–1969) brought the matter to the UN and used diplomatic pressure to force the Anglo-French-Israeli forces to withdraw. Egypt regained control of the canal while the UN deployed the first peacekeeping force in the organization's history. The UN force remained in the area until 1967. Two years later, a second force was deployed to Lebanon in response to a civil war that led to U.S. military intervention.

The Belgian Congo

In 1960, the UN sent a peacekeeping force to the Belgian Congo in an effort to end the country's civil war. After the former colony gained independence in 1960, Belgian troops remained and became involved in a civil war in the new country, where they supported the secessionist Katangese forces in the southern portion of the nation. In an effort to end the conflict, the UN deployed a peacekeeping force that eventually numbered 20,000. The force remained until 1964 and helped end the Katangese independence movement. UN Secretary General Dag Hammarskjöld (1905–1961) died in a plane crash while traveling to negotiate during the fighting.

THE UN AND COLD WAR TENSIONS

The UN was often used by the superpowers as a forum to achieve their goals. For instance, in 1962, after the discovery of Soviet missiles in Cuba, the United States confronted the Soviets at the UN Security Council with photographic evidence. The incident initiated the Cuban Missile Crisis, which almost brought the United States and the Soviet Union to war. After the Soviets agreed to withdraw the missiles in October 1962, the UN oversaw the dismantlement of the weapon sites.

After notable peacekeeping successes, the prestige of the UN suffered a setback when Egypt forced the withdrawal of UN peacekeepers from the Sinai following the end of the Six Day War. The UN increasingly lost its credibility as a neutral mediator. Both the United States and the Soviet Union blocked resolutions harmful to its interests or those of its allies. For example, it was not until 1970 that the United States vetoed its first UN Security Council resolution (regarding Rhodesia); however, beginning in 1972, the U.S. began vetoing resolutions that condemned Israel (the United States subsequently vetoed more than 30 other resolutions to protect Israel). The Soviet Union (and later Russia) has been the most frequent user of the veto, with more than 123 by 2007 (compared with 82 for the United States; Great Britain, 32; France, 18; and the PRC, 6).

With the end of the cold war in 1989, the UN gained greater relevance in international peace and security efforts. Even at the height of the superpower struggle, the UN provided badly needed food, medicine, and other supplies to the needy around the world. For instance, the World Food Program, founded in 1962, supplied food for 5 million refugees who returned to Algeria in its first year of existence. Throughout the 1990s, the UN expanded peacekeeping missions with the support of the former superpowers, including operations in Somalia, Haiti, and Sudan. The world body also undertook an increasingly active role in issues such as climate change.

Gavin Wilk

ADLAI STEVENSON (1900–1965)

Adlai Stevenson was an American politician and diplomat who gained notoriety during the early years of the cold war. Stevenson assisted in the creation and development of the Charter of the United Nations and was one of the first members of the American delegation to the UN. He served as the governor of Illinois from 1948 to 1952 and ran two unsuccessful presidential campaigns in 1952 and 1956. In 1961, President John F. Kennedy appointed Stevenson American ambassador to the UN. Stevenson would serve in this role until his death in 1965.

GUIDED READING

Ambrose, Stephen E. *Rise to Globalism: American Foreign Policy Since 1938.* New York: Penguin Books, 1997.

LaFeber, Walter. *America, Russia, and the Cold War, 1945–1990.* New York: McGraw Hill, 1991.

Meisler, Stanley. *United Nations: The First Fifty Years.* New York: Atlantic Monthly Press, 1995.

The United Nations. http://www.un.org.

United Nations. *A More Secure World: Our Shared Responsibility—Report of the Secretary-General's High-Level Panel on Threats, Challenges and Change.* New York: United Nations Press, 2004.

Urquhart, Brian. *Ralph Bunche: An American Life.* New York: W.W. Norton, 1993.

THE TRUMAN DOCTRINE

Announced by President Harry Truman on March 12, 1947, the Truman Doctrine promised American support for "free peoples" facing internal or external subversion. Truman's announcement marked an important step in linking the United States to postwar Europe's defense, and it signaled a U.S. commitment to opposing the advance of communism.

During World War II, in expectation of ultimate victory, Allied leaders discussed the postwar settlement. The leaders of Great Britain, France, the Soviet Union, and the United States hoped to continue their alliance during the postwar period, but several problems—including mutual mistrust—had arisen during the course of the war. A number of factors contributed to the climate of suspicion that continued once the war ended. One factor was that despite agreement among Allied leaders that they would accept nothing short of their enemies' unconditional surrender, the United States and Britain feared that the Soviet Union would sign a separate peace deal with Nazi Germany. At the same time, Soviet leader Joseph Stalin feared that the United States and Britain would seek a similar settlement.

Stalin's intention to install Communist regimes in Eastern Europe conflicted with the Anglo-American desire that elected governments take power. Stalin promised, and at first allowed, relatively free elections in nations occupied by the Red Army in 1944 and 1945, but it soon became clear that local Communist parties—backed by the Soviet Union—were attempting to take power.

In addition, Stalin resented the exclusive American possession of the atomic bomb. U.S. officials hoped that monopoly would make the Soviet leader susceptible to diplomatic pressure on all issues related to postwar settlements in Asia and Europe.

SPHERES OF INFLUENCE

In October 1944, Stalin and British Prime Minister Winston Churchill met face to face in Moscow and agreed that southeastern Europe would be divided into spheres of influence. Neither Britain nor the Soviet Union would for-

mally rule over any nation, but each would exert influence informally, and the governments within each sphere would be friendly toward the dominant power. Specifically, Stalin agreed that Greece would be in the British sphere, while Churchill agreed that Romania and most of Bulgaria would fall in the Soviet sphere. Influence over Yugoslavia and Hungary would be divided evenly. The two leaders, however, did not determine how the arrangement would be worked out in practice.

During World War II, Greece was occupied for some time by the German army. Several Greek resistance groups had formed to fight the occupiers, while the Greek government waited in London in exile for its chance to return. One major Greek resistance group was Communist-dominated (ELAS, or National People's Liberation Army), backed by the Soviet Union and Communist forces in neighboring Albania, Yugoslavia, and Bulgaria. Following the end of the German occupation in October 1944, all Greek factions agreed to respect the authority of the exiled government. In December 1944, however, differences between the Communists and their rivals exploded in a brutal civil war.

By Allied agreement, Great Britain had been given responsibility for the military liberation and occupation of Greece. With the outbreak of civil war, Britain supported the Greek government. Damage from years of war in Greece was extensive. Roads, railroads, and waterways had been neglected for years or devastated by bombing. Communication networks had been destroyed, and virtually the entire Greek merchant marine had been sunk. Inflation soared as food and other necessities became scarce. The weak and divided Greek government could do little to meet the country's enormous reconstruction needs.

The United States had been sending considerable amounts of material assistance to Greece, mainly foodstuffs and some economic aid, and the new United Nations had also provided temporary emergency relief. Nevertheless, Great Britain had been bearing the primary responsibility of restoring political order and economic stability to the country, and, given its own wartime losses and the burdens of defending its global empire, it could no longer afford to send aid to either the Greek or the Turkish governments. As a result, on February 24, 1947, Lord Inverchapel (1882–1951), the British ambassador in Washington, D.C., notified the U.S. government that his country would be unable to continue supporting Greece and Turkey after March 31.

U.S. Response

The British announcement came as no surprise to the U.S. government. For nearly two years, American officials had become increasingly concerned about the future of Greece, Turkey, and the entire Middle East. A year earlier, in 1946, U.S. and British officials working through the United Nations had pressured the Soviet Union to withdraw its troops from northern Iran. Aware of declining British power and civil strife in war-torn Greece, American policy makers reasoned that if Greece should fall to communism, Soviet influence could extend into the entire Mediterranean region.

U.S. officials were also concerned about Soviet attempts to pressure the Turkish government into concessions of territory and naval

THE TRUMAN DOCTRINE

On March 12, 1947, President Harry Truman addressed a joint session of Congress and requested aid to Greece and Turkey. He also announced the intention of the United States to support nations facing internal or external subversion—a policy that came to be called the Truman Doctrine:

"At the present moment in world history nearly every nation must choose between alternative ways of life. The choice is too often not a free one. One way of life is based upon the will of the majority, and is distinguished by free institutions, representative government, free elections, guarantees of individual liberty, freedom of speech and religion, and freedom from political oppression. The second way of life is based upon the will of a minority forcibly imposed upon the majority. It relies upon terror and oppression, a controlled press and radio, fixed elections, and the suppression of personal freedoms. I believe that it must be the policy of the United States to support free peoples who are resisting attempted subjugation by armed minorities or by outside pressures."

bases in the Dardanelles, a narrow, strategically important strip of water connecting the Black Sea and the Aegean Sea. By December 1946, U.S. Secretary of State James Byrnes (1879–1972) had concluded that both Greece and Turkey needed to be protected from subversion and that this would require a far more extensive American commitment than had been previously envisioned.

A dramatic expansion of aid would require approval from the U.S. Congress. American public opinion in late 1946 and early 1947 seemed generally positive toward the Soviet Union. The Republican Party, generally representing isolationist sentiment, had won control of Congress and was opposed to expanding American commitments abroad. Aware of these political currents, President Truman and his top advisors carefully courted congressional leaders, influential businessmen, newspaper owners, and radio stations. Their message was that the Soviet Union was attempting to extend its influence over three continents.

End to Subversion

On March 12, 1947, President Truman addressed a joint session of Congress and requested $400 million in aid for Greece and Turkey, pledging unspecified American support for "free peoples" threatened with internal or external subversion. Although he did not mention the Soviet Union by name, no one could mistake the target of his speech. On April 22 and May 8, the Senate and the House of Representatives, respectively, approved the aid request by large majorities. The media and public also responded favorably to Truman's speech. Some commentators noted parallels between the Truman Doctrine and the Monroe Doctrine, announced by President James Monroe (1758–1831) in 1823, which warned European powers not to interfere in the Western Hemisphere.

THE MARSHALL PLAN

Truman's speech had taken place while the foreign ministers of the United States, Britain, France, and the Soviet Union were holding meetings in Moscow to discuss Germany's future. After weeks of negotiating, however, no agreement had been reached. Seeking to break the impasse, U.S. Secretary of State George C. Marshall (1880–1959) met directly with Stalin. The Soviet leader seemed unconcerned about the lack of progress in establishing the future direction of Germany and other issues, prompting a frustrated Marshall to return to

President Truman signed the Foreign Aid Assistance Act, which provided foreign aid to Greece and Turkey. The provision of economic support to any nation resisting Communist pressure came to be known as the Truman Doctrine.

ARTHUR VANDENBERG (1884–1951)

*A*rthur Vandenberg was an influential U.S. senator from Michigan from 1928 to 1951. A former reporter and editor of the Grand Rapids *Herald*, Vandenberg became active in local Republican Party politics and was elected to four terms in the U.S. Senate. A staunch isolationist until the Japanese attack on Pearl Harbor in 1941, he became a champion of greater American engagement in international affairs. Toward that end, he worked closely with President Harry Truman and his top advisors in the years after World War II. As chairman of the influential Senate Foreign Relations Committee (1947–1948), Vandenberg lent crucial support to the passage of President Truman's request for aid to Greece and Turkey and the much larger request for aid to Europe that became the European Recovery Program, or the Marshall Plan.

Washington. Upon his arrival home, Marshall instructed his associates to draw up a plan for a comprehensive U.S. economic aid package to Europe. It became known as the European Recovery Program (ERP), or Marshall Plan. As in the case of aid to Greece and Turkey, the Truman administration succeeded in convincing Congress to fund the Marshall Plan. Greece did not fall to communism, and the Soviet Union was never able to pressure the Turkish government into conceding its territory or naval bases. Following Truman's speech and the announcement of the Marshall Plan, relations with the Soviet Union deteriorated further. With the four key Allies unable to reach agreement on the fate of Germany, the country was divided into two sovereign states in 1949—the democratic Federal Republic of Germany (or West Germany) and the Communist German Democratic Republic (East Germany). The United States henceforth became committed to a policy of "containing" the Soviet Union's influence worldwide.

Steve Remy

GUIDED READING

Bostdorff, Denise M. *Proclaiming the Truman Doctrine: The Cold War Call to Arms.* College Station, TX: A&M University Press, 2008.

Gerolymatos, Andre. *Red Acropolis, Black Terror: The Greek Civil War and the Origins of Soviet-American Rivalry, 1943–1949.* New York: Basic Books, 2004.

Jensen, Kenneth M., ed. *Origins of the Cold War: The Novikov, Kennan, and Roberts "Long Telegrams" of 1946.* Washington, DC: United States Institute of Peace, 1991.

Leffler, Melvyn P. *A Preponderance of Power: National Security, the Truman Administration, and the Cold War.* Palo Alto, CA: Stanford University Press, 1992.

THE MARSHALL PLAN

The Marshall Plan was a U.S. economic aid program—formally designated the European Recovery Program (ERP)—that provided $13 billion to 18 European nations and territories between 1948 and 1952. The ERP was a crucial component of the growing American commitment to economic stability and military security in postwar Europe.

In the months after the end of World War II, newspapers and newsreels around the world showed horrific scenes of destruction. Countries that had remained neutral during the war, such as Ireland, Spain, Switzerland, and Sweden, suffered little damage, but most nations in Europe faced a daunting task of recovery. At the same time, a number of countries were politically and socially unstable. Civil conflicts that had erupted during the war in Greece, Yugoslavia, and Italy, for example, threatened to continue—or did continue—into the postwar period. In France and Italy, Communist parties stood poised to gain millions of votes and possibly come to power democratically as new or restored governments struggled to cope with the war's aftermath.

TOWARD A EUROPEAN RECOVERY PROGRAM

In the immediate postwar period, individual European nations made impressive progress in repairing physical damage to roads, bridges, and railway systems. But the housing shortage remained an overwhelming problem, and black markets for food and basic goods proliferated. To complete the rebuilding of their economies, European nations thus needed to import goods—especially food, raw materials, and machinery—mainly from the United States. The problem was obtaining the money—dollars, specifically—needed to purchase U.S. goods. European producers had very few commodities they could export to U.S. markets in order to earn the dollars they needed to import goods from the United States. Short-term loans the United States gave to European nations were insufficient to address what was known as the dollar gap. To make matters worse, the winter of 1946 through 1947 in Europe was the most severe in memory, and millions were without adequate shelter.

The worsening economic situation in Europe threatened to destabilize politics across the

Women in the Soviet-controlled sector of postwar Berlin work to clear rubble by hand in July 1945.

continent. Many western European leaders and a growing number of U.S. officials feared that the Communist Party, under the control of the Soviet Union, would take advantage of the slow pace of reconstruction and the resulting hardship, and gain popular support—perhaps even come to power—in France, Italy, or elsewhere.

Meanwhile, relations among the Allies had been deteriorating. Nearly two years after the end of the war in Europe, no agreement had been reached regarding Germany's future—a crucial issue, given the importance of Germany's output to the larger European economy. Increasingly, U.S. officials understood that the German economy would have to be rebuilt quickly, but the prospect of German recovery so soon after the war's end made many Europeans nervous. In the view of all the Allies except the Soviet Union, a final peace treaty that included an agreement on a new, democratic constitution for Germany would be a necessary precondition for economic reconstruction. Fearing that the economic situation in Europe would worsen if negotiations over Germany dragged on, U.S. and British officials were increasingly willing to contemplate a formal division between their occupation zones and the zone administered by the Soviet Union.

A final peace treaty with Germany was never concluded in the crucial postwar years. In March 1947, U.S. Secretary of State George C. Marshall traveled to Moscow for a meeting with his French, British, and Soviet counterparts to discuss Germany's future. Toward the end of the month-long meeting, with no progress having been made, Marshall appealed directly to Soviet leader Joseph Stalin to break the impasse. He made no response. Marshall returned to the United States convinced that the government would have to act quickly to assist economic recovery in Europe. Back in Washington, Marshall instructed his top advisors to outline a comprehensive economic aid proposal.

Marshall's advisors assumed that the global economic depression of the 1930s had fueled both communism and fascism, and that the triumph of fascism in economically depressed Germany had led directly to World War II. The policy makers concluded that prosperity and peace in Europe would require individual European nations to abandon traditions of nationalism in favor of closer cooperation,

particularly on economic matters. On June 5, 1947, Marshall gave a speech at Harvard University's graduation ceremony in which he called attention to the slow pace of recovery in Europe and its possible consequences. While the United States stood ready to lend assistance, Marshall stated, the initiative must come from Europe. Nations there had to set aside their national prejudices and cooperate for the benefit of the entire continent.

President Harry Truman, Secretary of State Marshall, and many other American officials were convinced that Europe was in need of large amounts of U.S. aid. In terms of economic resources, the United States could easily afford a large aid package. The United States had suffered no physical damage during the war, while wartime demand had revived the American economy. By 1945, with all its major economic competitors in Europe and Asia ravaged by war, the United States was the world's only true economic and military superpower.

Congress and the American public would also have to be convinced. Many Americans, including members of Congress, did not believe that the United States should become entangled in Europe's affairs. Nonetheless, Marshall and Undersecretary of State Dean Acheson (1893–1971) worked closely with Republican Party leaders such as Arthur Vandenberg, chairman of the powerful Senate Foreign Relations Committee, to secure passage of the European Recovery Act in April 1948.

ADMINISTERING THE PLAN

Through the European Recovery Program, the United States offered aid to any European nation that requested it. Stalin, suspicious of U.S. intentions, rejected Soviet participation in the ERP and barred any Eastern European government from accepting aid. Eighteen European

GEORGE C. MARSHALL (1880–1959)

George C. Marshall was born in Uniontown, Pennsylvania, in 1880. He attended the Virginia Military Institute and was commissioned as an officer in 1902. During World War I, he served on the western front in France, where he demonstrated abilities as a planner. By 1939, he had been promoted to the rank of general and was appointed Chief of Staff of the U.S. Army. Although Marshall's contribution to the American war effort was perhaps his greatest achievement, he is best known as the architect of the European Recovery Program, or Marshall Plan. Concerned about the slow pace of reconstruction in postwar Europe and the lack of productive negotiations with the Soviet Union over Germany's future, Marshall called on the U.S. Congress to fund a massive economic aid program. The European Recovery Program became the most successful aid program of its kind in history. In recognition of this achievement, Marshall was awarded the Nobel Peace Prize in 1953.

At Harvard University's annual graduation ceremony on June 15, 1947, U.S. Secretary of State George C. Marshall called for a comprehensive American program to aid economic recovery in war-torn Europe:

"In considering the requirements for the rehabilitation of Europe, the physical loss of life, the visible destruction of cities, factories, mines, and railroads was correctly estimated, but it has become obvious during recent months that this visible destruction was probably less serious than the dislocation of the entire fabric of European economy. ... But even given a more prompt solution of these difficult problems, the rehabilitation of the economic structure of Europe quite evidently will require a much longer time and greater effort than had been foreseen. ... Europe's requirements for the next three or four years of foreign food and other essential products—principally from America—are so much greater than her present ability to pay, that she must have substantial additional help or face economic, social, and political deterioration of a very grave character. ... It is logical that the United States should do whatever it is able to do to assist in the return of normal economic health in the world, without which there can be no political stability and no assured peace. Our policy is directed not against any country or doctrine but against hunger, poverty, desperation, and chaos."

states and territories under Soviet domination did not accept the U.S. offer.

Less than two weeks after Marshall's speech at Harvard, the British and French governments convened a working group made up of representatives from 16 European states. They met from June through September to formulate responses to Marshall's announcement. In April 1948, the group became known as the Organization for European Economic Co-operation (OEEC), a multinational body responsible for supervising the distribution of Marshall Plan aid and coordinating the efforts of participating nations.

In the United States, meanwhile, President Truman created the Economic Cooperation Administration (ECA) and appointed Paul Hoffman, head of the Studebaker automobile company, as its chief administrator. ECA missions were established in each participating European nation to work with local governments in distributing U.S. aid. One of the ERP's innovations was the creation of counterpart funds in each participating nation. The closing of the dollar gap was a high priority early on, and counterpart funds allowed European producers to purchase American materials and equipment with local currency. Thus, European central banks were able to reinvest their respective currencies into their own national economies, hence closing the dollar gap and speeding recovery.

The American hope for a more integrated economic structure in western Europe met with some initial resistance in Europe itself, particularly in Great Britain, a country that had long resisted entanglements in economic and diplomatic affairs on the continent. A few farsighted European leaders saw the opportunity not only to repair war-related damage, but also to restructure and modernize their nations' economies. During the war, a few European government officials had advocated a postwar federation of European states in which economic and even political decisions would take place in a democratically elected, pan-European union. Both American and European advocates of closer European economic cooperation seized upon the ERP as a way to build momentum for European unification.

MARSHALL PLAN COUNTRIES, 1950

IMPACT AND INFLUENCE

Between 1948 and 1952, the United States provided $13 billion in aid under the Marshall Plan (about $740 billion today). This amounted to 5.4 percent of the gross national product of the United States in 1947. The program succeeded in closing the dollar gap and allowed aid recipients to purchase vital supplies and foodstuffs from the United States, while simultaneously encouraging closer cooperation—and therefore political reconciliation—between former enemies, especially France and Germany. The ERP accelerated European economic recovery efforts already well underway and helped set the stage for the creation of the European Economic Community, today known as the European Union.

The United States did not dictate how the aid must be spent, and few Europeans regarded the program as an effort by the United States to dominate their economies or influence their national politics. To the contrary, the Marshall Plan encouraged Europeans to believe that the United States would not abandon the continent in peacetime, as it had done after World War I. Nor was the ERP intended primarily to benefit the American economy; European markets were not nearly as important to American manufacturers as domestic markets. By the early 1950s, the United States exported only a small percentage of its goods to western Europe, and its investments there remained relatively small.

Perhaps the most important U.S. consideration in setting up the Marshall Plan was strategic. Reasoning that Communist governments might come to power if economic conditions did not improve quickly, U.S. policy makers had concluded that western Europe's quick economic recovery was essential to American national security interests. Policy makers feared that if Communist governments came to power in nations such as France, Italy, and Greece, the Soviet Union would wield preponderant political and economic influence over most of Europe. Along with the announcement of the Truman Doctrine in March 1947 and the establishment of the North Atlantic Treaty Organization (NATO) in 1949, the Marshall Plan signaled to the world a firm U.S. commitment to containing the spread of communism.

The American architects of the ERP did not believe that it could be replicated in other

places. Nonetheless, the Marshall Plan was so successful that it continues to inspire large-scale economic aid programs around the world to the present day. For example, the Marshall Plan was a direct inspiration for the Alliance for Progress, a program initiated by President John F. Kennedy in 1961 to encourage economic development and political democracy across Latin America. Decades later, in the 1980s, Senator Al Gore (1948–) used the Marshall Plan as a model for the Global Marshall Plan, a program for saving the global environment while maintaining the world economy.

Steve Remy

Austrian farmers load hay in August 1947 onto a harvester provided by Marshall Plan funds.

GUIDED READING

Behrman, Greg. *The Most Noble Adventure: The Marshall Plan and the Time When America Helped Save Europe.* New York: Free Press, 2007.

Gaddis, John Lewis. *The Cold War: A New History.* New York: Penguin, 2005.

Gordon, Lincoln. *A New Deal for Latin America: The Alliance for Progress.* Cambridge, MA: Harvard University Press, 1963.

Hogan, Michael J. *The Marshall Plan: America, Britain, and the Reconstruction of Western Europe.* New York: Cambridge University Press, 1987.

Milward, Alan S. *The Reconstruction of Western Europe, 1945–1951.* Berkeley: University of California Press, 1984.

Raucher, Alan R. *Paul G. Hoffman, Architect of Foreign Aid.* Lexington, KY: University Press of Kentucky, 1985.

Schain, Martin, ed. *The Marshall Plan: Fifty Years After.* New York: Palgrave, 2001.

THE RECOGNITION OF ISRAEL

U.S. debate over the prospect of a Jewish state in Palestine pitched domestic politics against international security. The issue was finally decided in 1948 with President Harry Truman's controversial decision to recognize the new state of Israel, creating a future U.S. ally and fueling anti-Americanism in the Middle East that has endured to the present day.

What should happen to the land between the Mediterranean Sea and the Jordan River has been a political hot potato for much of history. In the early twentieth century, as Arab and Jewish nationalist groups struggled to control of the area commonly known as Palestine, Great Britain stepped in with promises to both. The Ottoman Empire controlled the region at that time, and the British hoped to create new allies that would help them in their fight against the Ottoman Empire during World War I. In the McMahon–Hussein correspondence of 1915 and 1916, the British promised Arab rule of some Ottoman territory in exchange for leading an Arab revolt against the Ottoman Empire. In the Balfour Declaration, the British solicited support from Jewish, Zionist allies with the promise of support for a Jewish homeland in Palestine.

DEBATING A JEWISH STATE

The British promises to Arabs and Jews culminated in the November 1917 Balfour Declaration, named after British Foreign Secretary Arthur Balfour (1848–1930). According to that policy statement, the British government would view "with favour the establishment in Palestine of a national home for the Jewish people, and will use their best endeavours to facilitate the achievement of this object."

After World War I, the League of Nations bestowed Palestine to the British as a mandate for administration. During the mandate years, nationalist fighting took place between the Arabs and Jews in Palestine, and each faction also committed violence against the British administration. After years of trying to manage the conflicts, Great Britain issued the White Paper of 1939, declaring that it would leave Palestine within 10 years and that the Balfour Declaration was null and void.

U.S. Involvement

World War II was a major turning point in U.S. participation in the Middle East and the question of Palestine. The Holocaust increased American sympathies for the plight of Jews and the Zionist cause. In 1944, U.S. President Franklin D. Roosevelt authorized that it was acceptable for American Zionist supporters to profess future U.S. support for a Jewish national home in Palestine. Roosevelt met with Saudi King Ibn Saud (ca. 1880–1953) in 1945, offering aid and seeking his support for a Jewish state, but King Saud rebuffed the idea.

Roosevelt died shortly after his meeting with the Saudi king, and the new American president, Harry Truman, became embroiled in the question of Palestine. Truman's opinion was shaped by the horrors of the Holocaust, domestic lobbying from within the Zionist movement and his Democratic base, and the pressure to act regarding an inflow of Jewish immigrants from war-torn Europe.

Truman sought to pressure the British into easing immigration restrictions on Jewish people entering Palestine. A joint Anglo-American Committee of Inquiry concluded in 1946 with a proposal that 100,000 Jewish refugees be allowed into Palestine and called for the establishment of a British trusteeship, which would lead to an eventual binational state comprised of Jewish and Arab provinces.

Resolution 181

In 1947, the beleaguered British submitted the Palestine problem to the new United Nations, vowing to withdraw its authority and rule by May 1948. The UN Special Committee on Palestine (UNSCOP), formed in April 1947, called for a two-state partition of Palestine into a Jewish state and an Arab state. It also called for

Jerusalem, a city with strong historical and religious significance for Jews, Muslims, and Christians, to become an international trusteeship. The Zionists reluctantly accepted the proposal, but the Arabs rejected it as an unjust usurping of Arab land.

President Truman embraced partition, partly because Zionists and sympathetic Christian organizations had barraged the White House with letters pressuring him to support a Jewish state. In October 1946, President Truman made the first public pledge by a U.S. president to support a Jewish state in Palestine. With the American position favoring partition, demonstrations throughout the Middle East led U.S. Undersecretary of State Dean Acheson to lament that the United States had replaced Britain as the most disliked power in the Middle East.

The U.S. State Department opposed partition, but Truman lobbied members of the United Nations to vote for the plan. On November 29, 1947, the General Assembly passed Resolution 181, calling for partition of Palestine into two states, one Jewish and one Arab, with Jerusalem set aside for trusteeship.

Response to the Resolution

Arabs, who thought the UN plan was both intrusive and patently unfair, immediately began preparing for war. Palestinian militias joined the Arab Liberation Army, an army of volunteers from different Arab countries, in skirmishes against Jewish forces.

At first, Zionists accepted Resolution 181, but starting in December 1947, Zionist militias seized villages assigned to the Arabs. Witnessing the emerging violence, the U.S. State Department announced an embargo on arms shipments to Palestine and Arab states in December 1947. Truman pondered the wisdom of backing Resolution 181, and questioned whether to follow through with it or produce a workable alternative.

U.S. Secretary of State George Marshall urged Truman to reconsider the American commitment to the partition plan and a Jewish state in general. Marshall and a majority of diplomats at the United Nations viewed a direct UN trusteeship following the British mandate as the only viable solution to halt the bloodshed. The State Department urged Truman not to grant diplomatic recognition to the Jewish state of

Israel, but instead to promote the notion of a trusteeship. In March 1948, the U.S. delegation to the United Nations asked the Security Council to suspend action on partition and to convene a special session to consider a trusteeship.

Truman faced a domestic backlash as discussions in the United Nations dragged on and the mid-May deadline of British withdrawal approached. On May 12, 1948, a heated discussion occurred in President Truman's Oval Office. Marshall argued that the United States should support the idea of a trusteeship and defer any decision on recognition. Others cited the Balfour Declaration, the Holocaust, and the possibility of establishing a democratic nation in supporting an independent Israel.

Truman reassured Marshall he was on his side. Truman then wrestled with his options over the next two days. On May 14, 1948, the day the British mandate expired, Israel declared an independent state in Palestine. A mere 11 minutes later, under pressure from lobbyists, Truman formally recognized the new Jewish state.

President Harry S. Truman (*left*) holds a Torah presented to him by the president of Israel, Chaim Weizmann (*right*).

CONSEQUENCES OF RECOGNITION

While Israel would have declared independence anyway, and may have survived and persisted regardless of American influence, U.S. recognition and support for partition helped legitimate and strengthen the Jewish state's cause. It also inflamed the region and tied the United States to Israel's actions in the Middle East. Such consequences would have implications for U.S. foreign policy for decades to come.

THE NEW STATE OF ISRAEL

Truman's decision to recognize the new Jewish state was communicated in a White House press release just 11 minutes after Israel's declaration of statehood:

"This Government has been informed that a Jewish state has been proclaimed in Palestine, and recognition has been requested by the provisional government thereof. The United States recognizes the provisional government as the de facto authority of the State of Israel."

Implications for the Region

Israel's Arab neighbors mounted an assault on the newfound state the day after independence was announced, in what would be the first of several wars in the ongoing Arab-Israeli conflict. War led to the parceling of the would-be Arab state into areas absorbed or controlled by Israel, Egypt, or Jordan. The once promised Arab state in Palestine was forgotten for some time.

The 1948 Arab-Israeli War gave rise to the new and persistent issue of refugees. By the time of armistice in early 1949, Israel controlled 73 percent of Palestine, and as a result, an estimated 650,000 to 750,000 Arabs became refugees. In December 1948, UN Resolution 194 affirmed the "right of return" for Arab people expelled by war. With armistice, however, did not come peace. The warring parties chose instead a condition of "no war, no peace" for decades, occasionally punctuated by war (in 1956, 1967, 1973, 1982, and 2006) and by peace (Israel with Egypt in 1978 and with Jordan in 1994).

Implications for the United States

The U.S. relationship with Israel has always influenced its relationship with the rest of the Middle East. Distancing itself from the Jewish state under Truman and Eisenhower, the U.S.-Israeli relationship was strengthened in the 1960s, when the United States began to send aid and arms to Israel out of fear of radical Arab nationalism and Soviet expansionism. Starting in the 1970s, President Richard M. Nixon (1913–1994) and his successors referred to Israel as a strategic asset in the cold war. This positive relationship has extended into the post–cold war era.

Some consider Israel to be a liability when it comes to the reputation of the United States in the Arab and Muslim world. Others feel that Israel is an unjust state occupying Arab land, even well beyond the original vision of Resolution 181. Critics point to the domestic politics behind Truman's decision to recognize Israel. Truman himself suggested that the Palestine problem could have been solved if U.S. politics had been kept out of it.

Vaughn P. Shannon

These Palestinian refugees, pictured in 1948, lived in the corridor of a school building.

GUIDED READING

Ball, George W., and Douglas B. Ball. *The Passionate Attachment: America's Involvement with Israel, 1947 to the Present.* New York: W.W. Norton, 1992.

Brands, H.W. *Into the Labyrinth: The United States and the Middle East, 1945–1993.* New York: McGraw-Hill, 1994.

Mearsheimer, John J., and Stephen M. Walt. *The Israel Lobby and U.S. Foreign Policy.* New York: Farrar, Straus and Giroux, 2007.

Palestine Facts. http://www.palestinefacts.org.

Spiegel, Steven. *The Other Arab-Israeli Conflict: Making America's Middle East Policy, from Truman to Reagan.* Chicago: University of Chicago Press, 1985.

THE COLD WAR

The cold war was a struggle between the United States and the Soviet Union that lasted from the end of World War II to the early 1990s. The conflict divided the world into two rival blocs and was marked by limited, proxy wars between the two superpowers rather than a global war.

The Russian Revolution of November 1917 and seizure of power by the Bolsheviks led to the nation's withdrawal from World War I the following month and the founding of the Union of Soviet Socialist Republics (the USSR, or Soviet Union) in 1922. Drawing on the theories of Karl Marx (1818–1883), the leaders of the Soviet Union condemned capitalism as a system that exploited workers, and they believed workers should own the means of production. Politically, they advocated single-party rule, the abolition of private property, and world-wide revolution to create a global communist system.

The alliance between the United States and the Soviet Union during World War II was always uneasy, but faced with a larger threat from Nazi Germany the two sides cooperated. A number of disputes, however, emerged between the Allies. For example, Soviet leader Josef Stalin complained bitterly that Great Britain and the United States had taken too long to open a second front against the Germans in western Europe.

After the war, the Allies agreed to divide Germany into zones of occupation. The Soviets would continue to occupy areas of eastern and central Europe, but those countries would be allowed to conduct open elections and choose their own form of government. Stalin pledged not to interfere in western Europe. However, by fall 1945, it became clear that the Soviets intended to retain control over their conquered territory. Pro-Soviet regimes were installed and opposition groups were repressed. Meanwhile, the Soviets provided covert support to Communist insurgency groups in countries such as Greece and Italy that were supposedly outside of the Soviet sphere of influence.

THE IRON CURTAIN

On March 5, 1946, former British Prime Minister Winston Churchill spoke at Westminster College in Fulton, Missouri, where he introduced the term *iron curtain* to describe the Soviet control taking hold in Eastern Europe:

"From Stettin in the Baltic to Trieste in the Adriatic, an iron curtain has descended across the Continent. Behind that line lie all the capitals of the ancient states of Central and Eastern Europe. Warsaw, Berlin, Prague, Vienna, Budapest, Belgrade, Bucharest and Sofia, all these famous cities and the populations around them lie in what I must call the Soviet sphere, and all are subject in one form or another, not only to Soviet influence but to a very high and, in some cases, increasing measure of control from Moscow."

WAGING THE COLD WAR

After the war, the United States adopted the policy of containment, initially proposed by U.S. diplomat George Kennan in a 1946 telegraph. Containment was appealing to U.S. leaders because it offered a way to deal with the Soviets while avoiding another world war. However, containment also meant that the United States had to maintain military and economic pressure on the Soviet Union. In addition, the United States would remain actively engaged in world affairs. As part of the effort to reform the wartime military and increase efficiency, the National Security Act of 1947 created a new Department of Defense to coordinate U.S. military branches. It established a new intelligence body, the Central Intelligence Agency, and the National Security Council, which advised the president on foreign and security policy.

Europe and the Middle East were the initial "battlefields" of the cold war. Greece and Turkey were the initial recipients of assistance pledged by President Harry S. Truman as part of the Truman Doctrine, which pledged American economic and military aid to countries that faced Communist insurgencies. In order to contain the Soviets and their new satellite states in Eastern Europe, the United States undertook broad programs such as the 1947 Marshall Plan, which provided $13 billion in aid to the countries of western Europe in exchange for economic and political reforms. In 1949, the United States helped establish the North Atlantic Treaty Organization (NATO). NATO's mission was to deter Soviet aggression against western Europe by agreeing that an attack on any NATO country would be met with a response by every NATO country, including the United States. The United States demonstrated its commitment to freedom in Europe through its actions in Berlin when the Soviets cut off access to the Allied-controlled areas of the city. The United States initiated a massive airlift that delivered 2.3 million tons of food and supplies to the German city.

The Soviet Union responded to the Berlin Airlift by increasing political repression in areas under its control. It increased support for Communist insurgency groups around the globe, including in the French Asian colonies in Indochina. In addition, the Soviets provided weapons and supplies to Communists who took control of China in 1949. In response to NATO, the Soviets created a similar military treaty group, the Warsaw Pact, in 1955. Unlike NATO, which was focused on an external threat, the Warsaw Pact was used to maintain Soviet control. When Hungary attempted to democratize in 1956 and Czechoslovakia in 1968, Warsaw Pact forces were used to reassert Soviet control.

THE COLD WAR ON THE DOMESTIC AND CULTURAL FRONTS

The cold war had a tremendous impact on domestic politics and culture in the United States. Many Americans, often encouraged by the government, saw the cold war as a life and death struggle between two opposing worldviews. This led to an often-irrational fear that Communist agitators, taking orders directly from the Soviet Union, existed throughout the United States and threatened the American way of life. In the early 1950s, Senator Joseph McCarthy (1908–1957) of Wisconsin falsely claimed to have lists of Communists working

throughout the government. After a series of televised hearings a few years later exposed the senator's bullying tactics and baseless claims, the appeal of McCarthyism died down. However, thousands of Americans lost their jobs or suffered economic or political repression during the McCarthy era.

This 1955 image shows a man, woman, and child seated in "Kidde Kokoon," an underground bomb shelter.

Internationally, the United States launched a series of efforts to win over non-aligned countries, or nations not firmly under either the American or the Soviet sphere of influence. Because of the success of NATO, the United States created a similar organization in the Middle East, known as the Central Treaty Organization (CENTO), and in Asia, known as the Southeast Asian Treaty Organization (SEATO). All were designed to contain communism in their respective regions. The United States also created economic and humanitarian aid programs, including the 1961 Alliance for Progress that focused on Latin America and the 1961 Peace Corps. The Soviets countered with their own economic aid and programs by which youths in satellite countries or in developing states were educated in Soviet universities.

Both superpowers conducted covert operations and supported insurgents in efforts to undermine governments friendly to the opposing side. For instance, the CIA supported successful coups in Iran (1953), Guatemala (1954), and Chile (1973) to install pro-American governments. The Soviets supported successful insurgencies or coups in Cuba (1959), Ethiopia (1974–1977), and Grenada (1979).

HOT SPOTS

In addition to the ideological battles of the cold war, several instances of real war occurred between the superpowers and their proxies. In 1950, when the pro-Soviet North Korean Communist regime invaded the pro-United States South Korea, the United States used the UN to develop a coalition of 16 allied nations to fight the invading North Korean forces—and, later, Chinese and Soviet forces. The war lasted three years and took the lives of more than 2 million soldiers and civilians.

Also in the late 1950s, American involvement in South Vietnam began in an effort to prevent Communist North Vietnam from unifying the two former French colonies. The North Vietnamese were supplied and supported by the Soviet Union, which saw the conflict as a means to weaken the United States and undermine its military credibility. By the time the United States left in 1973, more than 50,000 Americans and more than 1 million Vietnamese had died.

Perhaps the most potentially dangerous episode of the cold war was the Cuban Missile Crisis. In 1962, the United States discovered that the Soviets had deployed missiles in Cuba, a Soviet ally. The incident almost brought the superpowers to war, before the Soviets agreed to remove the missiles. The Cuban Missile Crisis led to efforts to reduce tensions between the two global rivals, including the creation of the "red phone" whereby the leader of each country could communicate directly with his counterpart before events led to military escalation.

In 1979, the Soviet Union invaded Afghanistan. The United States supplied weapons and training for the anti-Soviet, Muslim Mujahideen, which waged a bitter war against the Soviet occupation. The Soviets withdrew in 1989, after 15,000 of its soldiers had been killed. More than 1 million Afghans perished as a result of the war.

THAW

When President Ronald Reagan (1911–2004) took office in 1981, he approved a series of military initiatives designed to push the teetering Soviet economy to the breaking point. That effort, combined with years of economic stagna-

East German guards standing atop the Berlin Wall watched as border crossings opened in 1989.

tion, led the Soviets to seek dramatic political and military reforms under Mikhail Gorbachev (1931–). Gorbachev's domestic reforms, known as *perestroika*, resulted in the liberalization of the Soviet economy. Countries in Eastern Europe began to push for greater political and economic autonomy in a process that accelerated when it became clear that the Soviets were not willing to use force to maintain control, as had been the case in the past. The Berlin Wall, separating Communist East Berlin from democratic West Berlin, came down in 1989. Soviet satellite countries began to declare their independence and dismantle their Communist regimes. The Soviet Union itself collapsed in 1991, following an abortive coup against Gorbachev, definitively ending the cold war.

John Day Tully

GUIDED READING

Cohen, Warren, ed. *The Cambridge History of American Foreign Relations. Vol. 4, America in the Age of Soviet Power, 1945–1991.* New York: Cambridge University Press, 1993.

Collier, Christopher. *The United States in the Cold War: 1945–1989.* New York: Benchmark Books, 2002.

Leffler, Melvyn P. *The Specter of Communism: The United States and the Origins of the Cold War, 1917–1953.* New York: Hill and Wang, 1994.

The National Security Archive. http://www.gwu.edu/~nsarchiv/.

Speakman, Jay. *The Cold War.* San Diego, CA: Greenhaven Press, 2001.

THE NORTH ATLANTIC TREATY ORGANIZATION

The North Atlantic Treaty Organization (NATO) is a mutual defense alliance established in 1949 to protect security in the transatlantic region. Today, it includes 26 North American and European member nations.

President Franklin D. Roosevelt and his successor, Harry Truman, were determined that the United States would not become isolationist after World War II. The urgency of American engagement in world affairs became increasingly apparent as the wartime alliance with the Soviet Union dissolved. In Eastern Europe, the gradual seizure of power by the Communist Party alarmed American and British officials. In the Middle East, Stalin attempted to keep Soviet troops in northern Iran (where they had been stationed during World War II) until American and British pressure forced him to withdraw them. Stalin also pressured the Turkish government for access to bases in the Dardanelles, a strategic waterway connecting the Black Sea to the Aegean Sea. Moreover, there was no agreement on a final peace treaty regarding defeated Germany, which the Allies divided into two separate states (democratic West Germany and Communist East Germany).

Postwar developments convinced American policy makers that the United States would have to remain engaged in western European affairs and would have to act to halt the spread of communism worldwide. In March 1947, President Truman pledged in the Truman Doctrine U.S. support for free countries facing internal or external subversion. Concerned about the political implications of slow economic recovery, the United States also provided $13 billion in aid to western European nations from 1948 to 1952, under the Marshall Plan.

Pledges of support and economic aid were not enough, however. Both American and western European leaders understood that they could not defend their nations without the help of the United States. The concept of a mutual defense alliance was largely a European initiative that found a receptive audience among American officials concerned about western Europe's security. Two crises in 1948 accelerated the creation of such an alliance. In February,

Stalin had authorized Communists in Czechoslovakia to overthrow the nation's democratically elected government. A few months later, the Soviet Union blockaded land routes into West Berlin, which lay in the Soviet occupation zone of Germany. (The city was divided among the four Allied Powers.)

To the leaders of western European nations, the Soviet actions reinforced the belief that Europe's future security required not only American economic aid and promises of support, but also a formal, mutual security treaty. Through mutual security, western European countries would be obliged to come to the defense of any treaty member that was attacked. A similar agreement, the Brussels Pact, had already been concluded between Great Britain, France, Belgium, the Netherlands, and Luxembourg in March 1948. Its main purpose was to deter an armed attack by any other nation or alliance.

Even as the negotiations for the Brussels Pact were taking place, British Foreign Secretary Ernest Bevin (1881–1951) stressed the importance of American involvement in western Europe's security to U.S. Secretary of State George Marshall. Marshall and other American officials, particularly Undersecretary of State Dean Acheson, were receptive to the idea of a North Atlantic security pact, and a series of secret negotiations began in Washington, D.C., between U.S., British, and Canadian officials with the objective of drafting a new agreement. In July 1948, other Brussels Pact members joined the negotiations, and by April 1949, NATO had been created. Its original members included the United States, Canada, the United Kingdom, France, Italy, Belgium, the Netherlands, Luxembourg, Norway, Iceland, Denmark, and Portugal.

West Germany was not one of NATO's original members, but farsighted American and European officials realized that it would have to be allowed to rearm and join the alliance. In late June 1950, with Stalin's approval, Communist North Korea launched an invasion into democratic South Korea. U.S. and western European officials feared the attack might be a kind of diversion, or perhaps the first stage in a global offensive coordinated by the Soviet Union, with West Berlin as the next target. Such fears made it possible to overcome any European resistance to West Germany's rearmament and admission to NATO, which took place in May 1955. The Soviets promptly responded by creating the Warsaw Pact, a treaty organization similar in many respects to NATO; the major difference was the near total lack of autonomy among non-Soviet member states.

STRUCTURE OF THE ALLIANCE

The North Atlantic Treaty created a mutual defense alliance among its member states. The heart of the treaty from the outset was Article 5, which states that an attack on one member state would be considered an attack on all member states. The treaty also provided for the creation of a governing body, or council, which became the North Atlantic Council.

The NATO alliance is headed by a secretary general who is appointed for a four-year term. All decisions taken by the council must be ratified unanimously. There is no formal NATO fighting force. Instead, individual members agree to commit their nation's armed forces as deemed necessary by the council. NATO's military commander, known as the Supreme Allied Commander Europe, or "SACEUR," is an American general. The first to hold the position was General Dwight D. Eisenhower, who served

in 1951 and 1952. NATO headquarters was located in Paris until 1966, when it was moved to Brussels.

NATO's initial strategy was based on the "forward defense" of western Europe, through which, in the event of war with the Soviet Union and the Warsaw Pact, NATO forces—including large numbers of U.S. troops stationed in western Europe—would engage in fighting with the enemy. Soviet ground forces outnumbered the combined ground forces of the NATO nations, and the alliance's architects understood that NATO was intended primarily to deter the Soviet Union from launching an invasion in the first place.

The North Atlantic Treaty also provided for the possibility of expanding the alliance. In 1952, Greece and Turkey were admitted, and West Germany became a member three years later. Spain, having made a successful transition to a liberal democracy after the death of the dictator Francisco Franco (1892–1975), joined the alliance in 1982. Germany "rejoined" NATO following the reunification of East and West Germany in 1990.

NATO SINCE THE COLD WAR

Beginning in fall 1989, a series of peaceful revolutions toppled Communist dictatorships in Eastern Europe. In 1991, the Soviet Union itself collapsed, bringing an end to the cold war. With the demise of the Eastern bloc came the demise of the Warsaw Pact. Some observers in the United States and Europe argued that NATO no longer had a purpose. Others believed it was important for NATO to continue. The nations of western Europe had never created a multinational military profile independent of NATO. In addition, the alliance was an important institutional link between the United States and Europe. So NATO was preserved, but its role changed.

Several initiatives during the 1990s expanded NATO's reach in Europe and beyond. In 1994, the organization created the Partnership for Peace, which has assisted non-NATO nations emerging from dictatorship to rebuild their armed forces. A year later, the Mediterranean Dialogue was created to improve relations and discuss common security interests with nations in North African and the Middle East. In 1997, NATO created two new bodies, the Permanent Joint Council (replaced in 2002 by the NATO-Russia Council) and the NATO-Ukraine Commission, to discuss security issues with those two former Soviet republics.

A series of civil conflicts in the former Yugoslavia provided the first opportunity for NATO forces to operate outside the North Atlantic region. NATO intervened in Bosnia and Herzegovina in 1995, in Kosovo in 1999, and in Macedonia in 2001. NATO forces have also had peacekeeping missions in Bosnia and Herzegovina, and in Kosovo.

When the United States was attacked by al-Qaeda on September 11, 2001, NATO invoked Article 5 of the North Atlantic Treaty for the first time in the alliance's history. Subsequently, 14 NATO allies deployed armed forces to Afghanistan and participated in the ensuing peacekeeping mission.

Since the end of the cold war, several Eastern European nations—including Poland, the Czech Republic, and Hungary in 1999, followed by Bulgaria, Romania, Slovakia, and Slovenia in 2004—and several former republics of the Soviet Union—including Estonia, Latvia, and Lithuania in 2004—have all joined the alliance.

The North Atlantic Treaty committed the United States to the long-term defense of western Europe. It further deepened the American presence in Europe and marked a break with past U.S. diplomacy, which avoided military alliances. NATO's first secretary general, Lord Ismay (1887–1965), remarked in 1952 that NATO's purpose was "to keep the Russians out, the Americans in and the Germans down." Having served that purpose throughout the cold war, NATO faced a new set of challenges after 1991 and continues to adapt to the challenges of the post–cold war world.

Steve Remy

GUIDED READING

Acheson, Dean. *Present at the Creation: My Years in the State Department*. New York: W.W. Norton, 1969.

Harry S. Truman Library & Museum. http://www.trumanlibrary.org.

Kaplan, Lawrence. *The Long Entanglement: NATO's First Fifty Years*. Westport, CT: Praeger, 1999.

North Atlantic Treaty Organization. http://www.nato.int.

Rupp, Richard. *NATO After 9/11: An Alliance in Continuing Decline*. New York: Palgrave Macmillan, 2006.

American occupation officials and American soldiers operating under NATO command speak with village elders in Zabul, Afghanistan, and prepare to hand out humanitarian aid supplies.

THE KOREAN WAR

On June 25, 1950, the Democratic People's Republic of Korea (North Korea), invaded the Republic of Korea (South Korea), initiating a conflict that spanned the next three years. It was the first major proxy war between the United States and the Soviet Union and their respective allies during the cold war.

In 1910, Japan annexed Korea, and the country would remain under Japanese control until the end of World War II, when Soviet troops invaded the northern part of the country. The United States and Soviet Union agreed to divide Korea in half along the thirty-eighth parallel at the end of the war. This was part of a broader effort on the part of the Soviet Union to increase territory under its control, and concurrent efforts on the part of the United States to promote democracy in order to counter Soviet expansion. Both the United States and the Soviet Union stationed troops in Korea, but Soviet forces left at the end of 1948, and American forces departed in June 1949. North Korea became a Communist dictatorship under the Soviet-backed leadership of Kim Il Sung (1912–1994), while South Korea was led by a pro-American regime headed by Syngman Rhee (1875–1965). Both the United States and the Soviet Union provided varying degrees of military and economic support to their respective client states.

INVASION OF SOUTH KOREA

North Korea's Kim Il Sung wanted to unify the peninsula and believed that he had the support of the Soviet Union to invade South Korea. He also mistakenly thought that the United States would not defend South Korea because of statements made by U.S. officials that South Korea and Formosa (Taiwan) were outside the perimeter that the United States would use force to protect.

North Korean troops streamed into South Korea on June 25, 1950, armed with Soviet-made tanks and weapons, in a surprise invasion. President Truman attempted to use the United Nations to stop the attack through diplomatic pressure. An emergency session of the Security Council was immediately called. The Security Council passed a U.S.-sponsored resolution that demanded the immediate withdrawal of North Korean forces from South Korea. Meanwhile, North Korea officially declared war on South Korea. The next day, South Korean government officials fled Seoul, the capital of South Korea, in anticipation of the advancing North Korean troops.

INTERNATIONAL COALITION

On June 27, the Security Council passed a resolution recommending that UN member nations provide assistance to South Korea. American warplanes began aerial attacks on North Korean forces, but they could not halt the advance, and North Korean troops captured Seoul. Three days later, General Douglas MacArthur, a U.S. general and World War II hero who assumed command of the American and South Korean forces, sent a telegram to U.S. officials, warning that South Korea was on the verge of destruction by Communist-led forces. MacArthur asked for the deployment of U.S. ground forces to stop the North Koreans.

A UN soldier assists a wounded Canadian rifleman to safer ground during the Korean War.

President Truman issued a statement about Korea on June 26, 1950,
in an effort to explain to the American people why he sought to
use the UN. He stated:

*"Our concern over the lawless action taken by the forces from North Korea,
and our sympathy and support for the people of Korea in this situation, are
being demonstrated by the cooperative action of American personnel in
Korea, as well as by the steps taken to expedite and augment assistance of
the type being furnished under the Mutual Defense Assistance Program.
Those responsible for this act of aggression must realize how seriously the
government of the United States views such threats to the peace of the
world. Willful disregard of the obligation to keep the peace cannot be
tolerated by nations that support the United Nations Charter."*

On July 7, the United Nations passed a resolution authorizing a unified UN coalition in South Korea led by the United States. Eventually, a total of 15 countries joined the effort in fighting against the North Korean forces: Australia, Belgium, Canada, Colombia, Ethiopia, France, Great Britain, Greece, the Netherlands, New Zealand, Turkey, South Africa, Luxembourg, the Philippines, and Thailand. The United States deployed almost 500,000 troops at the height of its commitment, and was the largest contributor to the UN forces outside of South Korea, which had 590,000 troops.

COMBAT OPERATIONS

By the end of July, the North Koreans controlled virtually the entire Korean Peninsula, with the exception of the southern port town of Pusan. On September 15, General MacArthur, who had been named commander of UN forces, unleashed a bold military plan. Approximately 70,000 American forces landed at Inchon, the port of Seoul, and quickly drove the North Koreans out of the capital city. By October 1, in a stunning turn of events, UN forces once again controlled South Korea.

The quick and decisive victory gave the American and UN forces hope of a united Korean Peninsula and an end to Communist rule in the north. On October 9, UN forces moved across the thirty-eighth parallel to fight the considerably weakened North Korean army. In an attempt to keep Communist China out of the war, Truman authorized the bombing of

bridges on the Yalu River, which separated North Korea from China.

On November 24, MacArthur sent UN forces north toward the Chinese border. The offensive proved unsuccessful and agitated the Chinese. Fearing that the U.S.-led forces might invade China in an effort to restore the Nationalist government, Communist Chinese leader Mao Zedong (1893–1976) authorized Chinese forces to enter the Korean Peninsula to fight the UN forces in November 1950. Eventually, more than 760,000 Chinese soldiers fought in Korea. The entry of the Chinese meant that the Soviets did not have to take a more active role in the fighting and could, instead, rely on their allies to engage in combat.

Chinese forces took UN troops by surprise and forced them to retreat southward in bitter fighting that was complicated by the Korean winter. Chinese and North Korean forces retook Seoul in January 1951. MacArthur urged President Truman to use greater force against the Chinese, including the potential use of nuclear weapons. Truman refused because he sought to avoid a direct war with China, and possibly the Soviet Union. By March, the UN forces were able to stop the Communist advance and recapture Seoul. They pushed the Sino-

SINO-SOVIET TREATY OF FRIENDSHIP, ALLIANCE, AND MUTUAL ASSISTANCE

In February 1950, the Soviet Union and the People's Republic of China signed a military alliance. Mao Zedong, the leader of the newly formed People's Republic of China, believed that an alliance with the Soviet Union was vital for his nation's interests and would provide a stabilizing force in the region against the United States and Japan. The agreement granted the Soviet Union continued use of the naval base at Luda in China's Liaonong Province. The Soviet Union in return gave China large amounts of military weapons, technological support, and machinery. As the Korean War broke out, Chinese assistance on behalf of the North Koreans solidified the alliance by allowing the Soviets to avoid direct involvement in the conflict.

Korean forces back to the thirty-eighth parallel. Meanwhile, relations between MacArthur and Truman deteriorated, due to the general's criticisms of the administration and his continuing calls for an escalation of the conflict. On April 11, the popular MacArthur was removed from command in a decision that undermined the president's domestic popularity. Truman eventually decided not to seek another term as president because of his low approval ratings, which were partially the result of his administration's management of the Korean War.

Having regained control of South Korea, Truman endeavored to negotiate an end to the conflict. Initially, the U.S. negotiators asked for all foreign troops to be removed from the Korean Peninsula. However, the Chinese launched a new offensive that was stopped by May. The war evolved into a stalemate along the thirty-eighth parallel, with neither side able to gain a significant advantage.

NEGOTIATIONS

General Matthew B. Ridgway (1895–1993), leader of the U.S. Eighth Army, succeeded MacArthur. New peace negotiations were initiated, but they were extremely slow, with disagreements focused on the handover of prisoners of war from both sides.

In 1952, the popular World War II hero General Dwight D. Eisenhower was elected president. During his campaign, the Republican Eisenhower had promised to end the Korean War. Weeks after winning the election in November 1952, Eisenhower secretly flew to Korea in an effort to revive the stalled peace negotiations. Eight months later, on July 27, 1953, the peace talks resulted in an armistice signed just south of the thirty-eighth parallel in Panmunjom, South Korea. Because he opposed the continuing division of Korea, Syngman Rhee refused to sign the armistice, which was,

General Matthew B. Ridgway was the commander of UN forces in Korea.

In December 1952, President-Elect Dwight D. Eisenhower travelled to Korea to inspect the UN and American troops.

instead, signed by the United States on behalf of the UN forces. The thirty-eighth parallel, which divided North and South Korea after World War II, would now serve as the demilitarized zone (DMZ) between the two countries. The DMZ still divides the two nations today and is guarded by a U.S. military force authorized by the UN.

THE FINAL TOLL

The Korean War resulted in more than 150,000 American casualties, including 54,000 killed. Approximately 400,000 Chinese were killed, along with more than 300,000 North Korean soldiers. Among the other nations with significant casualties, 58,000 South Korean soldiers were killed and more than 80,000 were missing in action, while the British lost more than 1,100, Turkey lost 720, and Canada lost 516. The Korean War was the first major armed conflict in the post–World War II era, and it set the stage for the cold war rivalry between the United States and Soviet Union, which would dominate international relations for decades to come. Although fighting has not resumed in more than six decades, the Korean Peninsula still remains deeply divided territory and a continuing source of diplomatic tension between the United States and China.

Gavin Wilk

GUIDED READING

Fehrenbach, T.R. *This Kind of War: The Classic Korean War History.* Washington, DC: Brassey's, 2000.

Halberstam, David. *The Coldest Winter: America and the Korean War.* New York: Hyperion, 2007.

Korean War Project. http://www.koreanwar.org.

McCullough, David G. *Truman.* New York: Simon & Schuster, 1992.

MCCARTHYISM AND GLOBAL ANTI-COMMUNISM

As communism took root in nations across the globe in the years following World War II, anti-Communist hysteria became widespread in the United States.

Although the United States and the Soviet Union had been Allies during World War II, their relationship soured in the years that followed, as the iron curtain descended on Eastern Europe. When World War II ended in 1945, the Soviet army moved quickly to control Eastern Europe, first by occupying Germany east of the Elbe River and then by intervening in Romania and Bulgaria to establish Communist-controlled governments. In 1947, the Soviets established Communist regimes in Hungary and Poland; in February 1948, Communists succeeded in ousting the government of Czechoslovakia and installing their own.

Tensions between the United States and Soviet Union intensified in June 1948, when the Soviets blockaded Berlin, a jointly administered city that lay within Soviet-occupied East Germany. The Western Allies were forced to bring in supplies by air during 1948 and 1949, in what became known as the Berlin Airlift. By the time the Soviet Union successfully tested its first atomic bomb in 1949, an event its former Allies in the West did not expect, the cold war was in full swing.

As communism was advancing across Eastern Europe, it was also gaining footholds in Asia. A civil war between Communists led by Mao Zedong and nationalists led by Chiang Kai-shek (1887–1975) raged between 1946 and 1949, ending with a Communist victory. Within months of the establishment of the People's Republic of China, Communist North Korean forces invaded South Korea in June 1950, starting a war that soon reached a stalemate.

AMERICAN ANXIETY

With the West seemingly powerless to stop Communist advancement, anxieties about communism reached a fever pitch among many Americans. For the second time in the twentieth century (after the late 1910s and early 1920s), a Red Scare took hold of the country. In March 1947, responding to Republican charges that the Democrats were soft on communism, Democratic President Harry Truman issued Executive Order No. 9835, which ordered a loyalty investigation for every federal job applicant to root out anyone suspected of communism affiliation. It also held agency heads responsible for the loyalty of their employees. The Civil Service consequently conducted about 3,000 investigations that resulted in the dismissal of 380 employees. Another 2,500 employees resigned because suspicions had been raised.

After Republicans gained control of the House of Representatives in the 1946 elections, the chairman of the House Un-American Activities Committee (HUAC) announced that there was a conspiracy in the film industry to overthrow the government. During the committee hearings that followed, 10 individuals called to testify claimed First Amendment rights and were later convicted of contempt of Congress. In the aftermath of the hearings, the major Hollywood studios pledged that they would not hire Communists or Communist sympathizers and created a "blacklist" of names. The list soon included New York's television industry as well,

After World War II, Josef Stalin sought to provide a protective cordon for the Soviet Union by establishing Communist control of Eastern Europe.

instilling fear and confusion among the accused. In 1948, the United States indicted and successfully prosecuted 11 officials of the Communist Party of the United States for violating the Smith Act (1940), which made it an offense to advocate or belong to a group that advocated the violent overthrow of the government.

Soon after the Hollywood hearings, HUAC heard testimony from Whittaker Chambers (1901–1961), a *Time* magazine editor, alleging that Alger Hiss (1904–1996), a former State Department official and head of the Carnegie Endowment for International Peace, had been a Soviet spy in the 1930s. Hiss soon went to trial, where he was convicted of perjury in 1950. That same year, after Great Britain arrested Klaus Fuchs (1911–1988), who had served on the Manhattan Project, for passing atomic secrets to the Soviet Union, the United States similarly

accused Harry Gold, Donald Greenglass, and Julius and Ethel Rosenberg of being Communist spies, executing the Rosenbergs in 1953.

MCCARTHYISM

In 1950, Republican Senator Joseph McCarthy (1908–1957) of Wisconsin gave a Lincoln's Day address in Wheeling, West Virginia, in which he emphatically claimed that he had the names of 205 (also reported as 57) "card-carrying Communists" in the State Department, a claim that later turned out to be groundless but at the time stirred anti-Communist sentiment. A short time later, McCarthy lodged accusations of Communist membership against Owen Lattimore (1900–1989), a China specialist at Johns Hopkins University, and Philip Jessup (1897–1986), the United States representative to the United Nations.

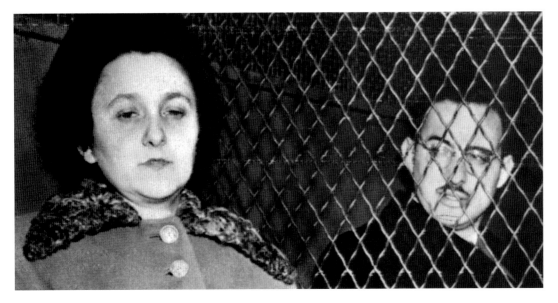

The United States executed Julius and Ethel Rosenberg in 1953 after their conviction for participation in an atomic espionage ring.

Senator Joseph McCarthy of Wisconsin held hearings to uncover Communists in institutions such as the Voice of America, the Government Printing Office, the Foreign Service, and the U.S. Army.

In response, the Senate established a committee under the leadership of Millard Tydings (1890–1961) of Maryland to investigate McCarthy's charges. When the committee concluded that the accusations were groundless, McCarthy launched a smear campaign against Tydings, who was defeated in his 1952 reelection campaign. Also in 1952, McCarthy became chairman of the Senate Committee on Government Operations. In this capacity, he conducted several investigations into alleged subversive activity, accusing anyone and everyone who disagreed with his tactics of being a Communist.

Efforts to weed out Communists spread beyond Senator McCarthy, further encouraging his campaign. In 1951, President Truman strengthened Executive Order No. 9835 by adding the stipulation that the burden of proof lay with the accused rather than with their accusers. The next year, the Immigration and Nationality Act tightened immigration quotas and allowed the deportation of foreigners deemed "detrimental" to the national interest. Other public organizations followed the federal government's lead, with the result that approximately 500 state and local government employees, 600 public school teachers, and 150 college professors lost their jobs because of loyalty concerns.

END OF THE RED SCARE

In 1954, McCarthy led an investigation into an alleged spy ring at a New Jersey army base. During Senate hearings held from April 22 through June 17, accusations flew back and forth between the U.S. Army and Senator McCarthy. Americans across the nation watched the hearings on television, seeing McCarthy's bullying tactics for the first time. Support for the Wisconsin senator and his mission fell dramatically. In July, Senator Ralph Flanders (1880–1970) of Vermont introduced a resolution to remove McCarthy from the government oper-

ations committee, later changing his resolution to one of censure. The Senate held hearings on McCarthy's alleged abuse of power, and in December 1954 voted to "condemn" him. McCarthy died in May 1957, apparently from the effects of alcoholism.

With McCarthy's fall, the second Red Scare passed its heyday and soon ran out of steam. The Communist Control Act (1954), which effectively outlawed the Communist Party and participation in it, was the last significant legislation of the second Red Scare. The anti-Communist tide ebbed with a series of Supreme Court decisions that took place from 1955 to 1957, concluding with *Yates v. United States*, which strengthened civil liberties and limited the government's investigative powers. Political power also had shifted to the Democrats, who had gained control of both houses of Congress in 1954.

The legal and political changes that strengthened civil liberties took place in part because international developments were reducing the anxiety that had produced the Red Scare in the first place. In 1953, an armistice ended the Korean War, and Joseph Stalin died. In 1955, the cold war thawed slightly when President Dwight D. Eisenhower met with Soviet Premier Nicolai Bulganin (1895–1975) in Geneva. Even the Soviet Union's crushing of rebellions in Hungary and Poland in 1956 was not enough to restart the anti-Communist crusade so passionately led by Senator McCarthy.

Gary Land

GUIDED READING

Caute, David. *The Great Fear: The Anti-Communist Purge Under Truman and Eisenhower.* New York: Simon & Schuster, 1978.

Fariello, Griffin. *Red Scare: Memories of the American Inquisition, An Oral History.* New York: W.W. Norton, 1995.

Reeves, Thomas C. *The Life and Times of Joe McCarthy: A Biography.* New York: Stein and Day, 1982.

Schrecker, Ellen. *Many Are the Crimes: McCarthyism in America.* Boston: Little, Brown, 1998.

Iran, Guatemala, and the CIA

During the 1950s, the Central Intelligence Agency (CIA) increasingly used covert operations to influence global politics. CIA operations toppled governments in Iran (1954) and Guatemala (1954) and installed pro-American regimes as part of the broader containment strategy of the United States.

In 1946, the American diplomat George Kennan (1904–2005) wrote what came to be called the Long Telegram. Kennan's ideas formed the basis for the cold-war policy of containment, whereby the United States avoided direct military confrontation with the Soviet Union and instead sought to prevent Moscow from gaining new allies or expanding its influence. Containment was based on the notion that the Soviet economic and political system could not be sustained indefinitely and was dependent on expansion and the acquisition of new satellite states. For containment to be effective, the United States had to maintain its allies. The policy was appealing because it would cost significantly less in economic terms—and in the lives of soldiers—than another world war.

THE NSC AND CIA

After World War II, a long period of decolonization and independence occurred throughout the world, as empires granted freedom to their global possessions or people overthrew hereditary or monarchial regimes. In some cases, such as in India (1947), independence was gained through negotiations, while in other cases, such as Algeria (1962), independence came after lengthy and bloody revolutions. The United States generally supported decolonization, and American officials hoped the new nations would emerge as democratic partners who would trade with America and join the global effort against communism.

Meanwhile, in 1947, the United States undertook a significant reform to its security infrastructure. The National Defense Act established two new organizations, the Central Intelligence Agency (CIA) and the National Security Council (NSC). The CIA was created in order to bolster the nation's civilian intelligence capabilities. The NSC was an advisory group that included the president, vice president, secretary of defense, secretary of state, the director of the CIA, and other government leaders as appointed by the president.

Following its creation, the CIA was initially led by career military officers, but in 1953, President Dwight D. Eisenhower appointed a civilian, Allen Dulles (1893–1969), to the post. Dulles was the brother of Secretary of State John

THE LONG TELEGRAM

The following excerpts are from the Long Telegram, sent by Diplomat George Kennan from the U.S. Embassy in Moscow to U.S. Secretary of State George C. Marshall on February 22, 1946, describing the political conditions in the Soviet Union:

"This political force has complete power of disposition over energies of one of world's greatest peoples and resources of world's richest national territory, and is borne along by deep and powerful currents of Russian nationalism. In addition, it has an elaborate and far flung apparatus for exertion of its influence in other countries, an apparatus of amazing flexibility and versatility, managed by people whose experience and skill in underground methods are presumably without parallel in history. ... Problem of how to cope with this force [is] undoubtedly greatest task our diplomacy has ever faced and probably greatest it will ever have to face."

Diplomat and historian George Kennan is credited as one of the creators of the U.S. containment policy during the cold war.

ALLEN DULLES (1893–1969)

Allen Dulles was the director of the CIA from 1953 to 1961. During World War II, he had served as office chief at the Office of Strategic Services (OSS), the main U.S. intelligence agency during World War II, in Berne, Switzerland. After the war, he became head of the OSS office in Berlin. Dulles was instrumental in the development of the CIA after its creation in 1947. In 1951, he was named deputy director of the intelligence agency, and in 1953, President Eisenhower promoted Dulles to director. As director, Dulles strongly believed in using the CIA as a tool in the containment of communism. Dulles argued that his agency could accomplish major U.S. policy objectives that would otherwise require the use of force. His use of covert operations in Iran and Guatemala set a dangerous precedent for the CIA, and the failure of the Bay of Pigs invasion in 1961 led to his resignation. He was the longest-serving CIA director in the organization's history.

Foster Dulles (1888–1959). The presence of both Dulles brothers on the NSC meant that they had an extraordinary influence on U.S. foreign and security policy. Both were staunch anti-Communists who advocated aggressive action to contain the Soviets.

POSTWAR IRAN

In April 1951, Mohammed Reza Pahlavi (1919–1980), the pro-Western shah of Iran, succumbed to popular pressure and appointed the nationalist leader Mohammed Mossadeq (1882–1967) as the prime minister of Iran. Mossadeq was a prominent figure in Iranian politics and de facto leader of the political group the National Front. He had been elected prime minister by the Iranian parliament. Mossadeq,

Mohammed Mossadeq, photographed here in 1951, was viewed as pro-Communist by U.S. officials.

however, was opposed by the shah because the National Front supported the abolishment of the monarchy and the nationalization of the country's oil industry, which was at that time was controlled by the British-run Anglo-Iranian Oil Company (AIOC). Three days after taking office, Mossadeq nationalized the AIOC. In response, the British imposed economic sanctions on Iran. The sanctions crippled the Iranian economy and the shah dismissed Mossadeq in 1952, but had to reappoint him after widespread public protests. The prime minister cut all official ties with Britain in October 1952.

Meanwhile, the United States became concerned with the growing popularity of the Tudeh Party, the Iranian Communist Party. The Tudeh Party and a conservative, Islamic party were key allies of Mossadeq's National Front in Iran's parliament. The Dulles brothers were concerned that the Iranian prime minister was reorienting the country away from the United States and toward the Soviet Union, following reports from the British that highlighted some of Mossadeq's more leftist policies. After Mossadeq's reappointment, parliament granted him emergency powers that allowed the prime minister to make some decisions without gaining legislative approval. The prime minister then reduced the power of the shah and initiated a program to redistribute land from the aristocracy to the poor. British officials suggested joint Anglo-American action to remove Mossadeq after the prime minister lost the support of Islamists in the parliament, forcing him to rely even more heavily on the Tudeh.

In April 1953, Allen Dulles allocated $1 million for a covert operation to remove Mossadeq. His goal was to replace Mossadeq with General Fazlollah Zahedi (1897–1963) as the leader of Iran. The CIA director had the support of his brother at the State Department, and Eisenhower quickly approved CIA action. The CIA and British intelligence began to spread anti-Mossadeq propaganda in Iran, while funds and weapons were provided to the Iranian military, which was pro-Zahedi. Facing external threats from the United States and Great Britain and a restive population chafing under economic sanctions, Mossadeq became increasingly dictatorial. He abolished the use of the secret ballot and then conducted a tainted referendum to abolish parliament. He also tried to force the shah into exile. In return, the shah again formally dismissed Mossadeq as prime minister, and wanted to appoint Zahedi in his place. Mossadeq refused to leave office, however, and the shah fled into exile on August 15. On August 19, 1953, pro-Zahedi forces took over government offices. They arrested Mossadeq on the following day. The shah returned from exile on August 22. He subsequently emerged as one of America's closest allies in the Middle East throughout the cold war. However, U.S. participation in the coup and support for the shah triggered anti-American sentiment in the region for generations.

POSTWAR GUATEMALA

The relative success of the Iran mission led the CIA to orchestrate another covert operation the following year, this time in Guatemala. In 1945, Juan Jose Arevalo (1904–1990) became the first democratically elected president of Guatemala. Arevalo's policies focused on the right to private property. The president introduced programs that strengthened democracy by expanding the right to vote and began numerous social programs, including the construction of houses, schools, and hospitals. However, some in the United States believed that Arevalo and his administration were sympathetic to the Communists. After serving a six-year term, Arevalo was succeeded in 1951 by his minister of defense, Jacobo Arbenz Guzmán (1913–1971).

In June 1952, Arbenz announced an agrarian reform bill that would redistribute uncultivated land from plantation owners to poor farmers. At the time 2.2 percent of the population controlled 70 percent of the land. The land identified for redistribution included 400,000 acres (162,000 hectares) of United Fruit Company (UFC) property. The UFC was an American-owned corporation that renounced the redistribution as a Communist plot to illegally give out land without fair compensation (the UFC had rejected the Guatemalan government's offer of $600,000 and instead asserted that the land was worth in excess of $15 million). The UFC lobbied U.S. officials for assistance. The State Department tried to mediate the dispute, but the Arbenz government refused to bow to U.S. pressure. The United States then implemented a series of economic sanctions on Guatemala. After the discovery that Arbenz had secretly met with members of the Guatemalan Communist Party while crafting his agricultural reforms, the Eisenhower administration again called on the CIA to secretly intervene.

Between $5 million and $7 million was allocated to a covert operation, and 100 American operatives were deployed to facilitate the removal of Arbenz from power. The CIA chose former Guatemalan military officer Carlos Castillo Armas (1914–1957) to lead the invasion from Honduras. The rebels were provided with rifles, ammunition, and several old American bombers. About 400 rebels also received military training in Florida. Pamphlets were dropped from aircraft throughout Guatemala, warning the population of an upcoming invasion. At the same time, CIA operatives worked with conservative, anti-Arbenz groups in Guatemala to undermine the government through propaganda and false media stories.

On June 18, 1954, around 450 troops, led by Armas, invaded Guatemala. Meanwhile, U.S. Marines conducted landing exercises in Honduras, leading many Guatemalan military officers to believe that the United States would use force to support Armas. Several senior military officers defected to Armas. On June 27, Arbenz, fearing the military would turn against him, resigned and fled the country. Before Armas could take power, other army officers attempted to take control of the country. After several days of political intrigue, Armas became president on July 8. He nullified the agricultural reforms of Arbenz and initiated a campaign to purge Communists in Guatemala. On July 26, 1957, Armas was assassinated. Although the CIA action effectively toppled the Arbenz government, the coup ultimately weakened the power of the central government of Guatemala and led to social and political unrest for decades to come.

Gavin Wilk

GUIDED READING

The Central Intelligency Agency. http://www.cia.gov.

Cleveland, William L. *A History of the Modern Middle East.* Boulder, CO: Westview, 1994.

Immerman, Richard H. *The CIA in Guatemala: The Foreign Policy of Intervention.* Austin: University of Texas Press, 1982.

Jonas, Susanne. *The Battle for Guatemala: Rebels, Death Squads, and U.S. Power.* Boulder, CO: Westview, 1991.

THE CIVIL RIGHTS MOVEMENT AND ANTI-COLONIALISM

As the civil rights movement took shape in the United States, it became increasingly clear that the struggles against legal racism in America and the movement for national independence from European colonization were linked, each providing inspiration and guidance to the other.

During the nineteenth and twentieth centuries, in the process of maintaining and controlling their overseas colonies, European powers often established a social order that elevated the status of "white" Europeans and denigrated "non-white" indigenous peoples. A similar racial order existed in the United States, where African Americans and other ethnic minorities endured legal subordination.

CONNECTING THE MOVEMENTS

For many years, most African Americans failed to connect the inequalities they endured with those faced by inhabitants of colonial societies. The few leaders who did make the connection proved influential. Civil rights activists such as W.E.B. Du Bois (1868–1963) and Marcus Garvey (1887–1940) attempted to connect the African American community with other peoples of African descent the world over through the ideal of Pan-Africanism. Nevertheless, early civil rights activist in the United States generally focused on ameliorating the problems of racism in America, rather than the existence of white supremacy in European colonies elsewhere.

The outbreak of World War II, however, caused the African American community to link racism at home with imperialism abroad. Italy's invasion, conquest, and colonization of Ethiopia in 1936 prompted considerable protest from African Americans, exposing a new level of awareness of the global nature of racial inequality. This awareness grew after America's entry into World War II, when the civil rights movement launched a "Double Victory" campaign against tyranny overseas and inequality at home. The Double Victory campaign focused on liberating not only the peoples oppressed by the Axis but also those subjugated by the colonial regimes of America's European Allies. The war being fought for freedom and democracy, civil rights leaders argued, must apply not just to Europe but to the entire world, including Europe's colonies. As Walter White (1893–1955), president of the National Association for the Advancement of Colored People, argued in his book *A Rising Wind* (1945): "The struggle of the Negro in the United States is part and parcel of the struggle against imperialism and exploitation."

World War II also marked a turning point for a number of independence movements seeking to overturn European colonialism. Early military victories by Japan against European colonies in Southeast Asia marked an important blow against the ideal of white supremacy. National movements soon sprang up across the world to secure independence against European rule. Independence movements resisted attempts by European powers to reestablish their power again after the war. Widespread conflict erupted as freedom movements broke out in places such as Algeria, Ghana, Indonesia, Kenya, Malaysia, and Vietnam.

The stance of the United States toward these battles for national independence was shaped by the early years of the cold war. The United States initially backed European powers, fearing that newly independent nations might succumb to the influence of communism and the Soviet Union. Both attracted the support of some national independence movements because both officially renounced the ideals of racism and white supremacy. Indeed communism's ideology of racial equality attracted a number of African American leaders, most notably W.E.B. Du Bois. However, the cold war created a split within the American civil rights community over the issue

of colonization. Leaders such as Du Bois advocated a message of international solidarity against racism and support for national independence. Other African American leaders toned down their rhetoric against colonization so as to maintain the support of the U.S. government, which was taking an increasingly supportive stand on the issue of civil rights.

COMBINED INFLUENCE

Over time, a number of anticolonial movements succeeded in gaining national independence. The United States reached out to these countries, wishing to avoid being diplomatically outmaneuvered by the Soviet Union. The civil rights community also embraced some of the techniques used by anticolonial activists to secure self-determination.

The influence of anticolonial activists on the civil rights movement was particularly noteworthy in the case of India. Mohandas K. Gandhi (1869–1948) was the leader of the Indian National Congress, an organization dedicated to ending British rule in India and establishing an independent nation. Gandhi pioneered the technique of nonviolent civil disobedience against the British authorities, which proved pivotal in the movement's success; India gained its independence from Britain in 1947. Gandhi's accomplishments gained international attention, not least among African Americans. As early as the 1920s, Garvey praised Gandhi and advocated the use of similar tactics by African Americans. The experience of the Indian independence struggle inspired and influenced members of the African American community

Members of the Congress of Racial Equality (CORE) staged a sit-in, a form of nonviolent civil disobedience, at the base of the Liberty Bell in Philadelphia in September 1963. They were protesting against racial prejudice in Alabama.

over the coming decades. Gandhi's influence was most profound on the Reverend Martin Luther King, Jr. (1929–1968), who first learned of the Mahatma and his tactics as a seminary student in 1950. Gandhi's example of nonviolence and his insistence on loving one's enemies deeply moved the Reverend King and provided a viable and peaceful means of overturning the racist order in the United States. King and his followers adapted Gandhi's methods to great effect in the African American struggle for freedom and equality during 1950s and early 1960s.

Civil rights leaders exercised nonviolent civil disobedience in numerous protests against racial segregation, often eliciting violent reprisals. The bravery and restraint demonstrated by protesters in the face of such violence resulted in international media attention. This, in turn, led government leaders to recognize racial prejudice as a diplomatic handicap during the cold war. Presidents John Kennedy and Lyndon Johnson advocated passage of federal legislation to end racial discrimination, paving the way for the Civil Rights Act of 1964 and the Voting Rights Act of 1965.

GANDHI'S INFLUENCE

The Civil Rights movement in the United States was inspired by Gandhi, whose Indian followers also engaged in nonviolent protest, such as breaking the law by evaporating salt from seawater, as shown in this image from the early 1930s.

Martin Luther King, Jr., was greatly influenced by the activism of Mohandas K. Gandhi. King wrote the following article on January 30, 1958, commemorating the tenth anniversary of the Mahatma's assassination:

"Mahatma Gandhi has done more than any other person in history to reveal that social problems can be solved without resorting to primitive methods of violence. In this sense he is more than a saint of India. He belongs—as they said of Abraham Lincoln—to the ages. In our struggle against racial segregation in Montgomery, Alabama, I came to see, at a very early stage, that a synthesis of Gandhi's method of nonviolence and the Christian ethic of love is the best weapon available to Negroes for this struggle for freedom and human dignity. It may well be that the Gandhian approach will bring about a solution to the race problem in America. His spirit is a continual reminder to oppressed people that it is possible to resist evil and yet not resort to violence. The Gandhian influence in some way still speaks to the conscience of the world as nations grapple with international problems. If we fail, on an international scale, to follow the Gandhian principle of nonviolence, we may end up by destroying ourselves through the misuse of our own instruments. The choice is no longer between violence and nonviolence. It is now either nonviolence or non-existence."

The changing attitudes of the United States and the accomplishments of civil rights activists inspired new efforts to overturn colonial regimes across the world. In 1957, Ghana became the first African nation to win independence. King and other civil rights leaders traveled to Ghana, where they joined anticolonial activists from throughout the world to celebrate the creation of the new nation. Dr. King's visit further connected the two movements, with each providing new inspiration to the other. By 1960, 18 new African nations had broken away from colonial rule, forming a wave of national self-determination that soon swept the globe. The struggle for freedom drew directly from the experiences of King and the African American civil rights movement.

The connection between the civil rights movement and anticolonialism continued during the 1970s and 1980s, most notably in South Africa. Under minority white rule, South Africa for decades had maintained a legal system of racial inequality known as *apartheid* (Dutch for "separateness"). The systematic repression of native peoples under apartheid generated a growing protest movement among South Africa's black majority—most the National African Conference, led by Nelson Mandela (1918–). The brutalities and injustice committed in the name of apartheid, including the 27-year imprisonment of Mandela, drew international condemnation and sparked a wave of activism in the African American community. The activism grew into a nationwide campaign in the 1980s that pressured universities and corporations to

pull investment money from South Africa and led to the passage of economic sanctions by Congress in 1986. Continued protests inside South Africa and mounting international pressure led by the African American community finally led to the release of Mandela in 1990 and the formal end of the apartheid regime in 1994.

Daniel Hutchinson

In October 1976, British stage and screen actors protested against the detention of political dissenters in South Africa.

GUIDED READING

Borstelmann, Thomas. *The Cold War and the Color Line: American Race Relations in the Global Arena.* Cambridge, MA: Harvard University Press, 2001.

Dudziak, Mary L. *Cold War Civil Rights: Race and the Image of American Democracy.* Princeton, NJ: Princeton University Press, 2000.

Harris, Robert L., and Rosalyn Terborg-Penn, eds. *The Columbia Guide to African American History Since 1939.* New York: Columbia University Press, 2006.

Kapur, Sudarshan. *Raising Up A Prophet: The African-American Encounter with Gandhi.* Boston: Beacon Press, 1992.

National Civil Rights Museum. http://www.civilrightsmuseum.org.

Noer, Thomas J. *Cold War and Black Liberation: The United States and White Rule in Africa, 1948–1968.* Columbia: University of Missouri Press, 1985.

THE SUEZ CANAL CRISIS AND ARAB NATIONALISM

From its opening in 1869, the history of the Suez Canal has been marked with conflict and political strife, peaking in the international Suez Crisis of 1956. The events of that year marked the end of British and French colonialism in the region and firmly pushed Egypt into the Soviet sphere for the next two decades of the cold war.

On July 26, 1956, Egyptian President Gamal Abdel Nasser (1918–1970) gambled against Western reprisal and nationalized the Suez Canal as part of a broader effort to take control of foreign-held enterprises in the country. The canal, for years a focal point in British-Egyptian tensions, represented the last vestige of British colonialism in Egypt.

The end of British rule had begun as early as 1945, and tensions culminated through increased British military presence and the declaration of martial law in 1952. One year after the tumultuous end of the nation's monarchy, Egypt and the United Kingdom signed a treaty on October 19, 1954, which set a two-year timeline for the withdrawal of British troops. Under pressure from the United States and with the timeline drawing near the end, the United Kingdom completed its withdrawal of 90,000 troops in June 1956, ending its 72-year occupation. Under the terms of the agreement, however, the canal was to remain under the control of the British- and French-owned Suez Canal Company.

ARAB NATIONALISM AND SOVIET TIES

Many in the Arab world, especially in Egypt, viewed the Suez Canal as a continuing symbol of the colonial past. Arab nationalism had led to a series of failed revolts against the colonial powers in the 1920s, but it was not until the 1950s, with the decline of British influence in the region and the French-Algerian War (1954–1962), that the nationalist movement blossomed.

With the Egyptian Revolution of 1952 and the consolidation of power under Gamal Abdul Nasser (1918–1970), Arab nationalism found a leader with broad appeal across the region. President Nasser initially found support from the United States and the United Kingdom in the form of development loans and other eco-

nomic assistance. At the same time, he developed increasingly close ties with the Soviet Union.

In September 1955, Egypt purchased military equipment from Bulgaria and Czechoslovakia, which were both Soviet satellite states. Nasser also ended diplomatic ties with the Chinese Nationalist government of Taiwan and recognized the Communist People's Republic of China. Moreover, Nasser's embrace of Arab nationalism led to fears in Washington, D.C., and London that he would support revolts against Western-backed regimes. Consequently, the United States and the United Kingdom withdrew financial support for several Western-backed Egyptian projects, including the Aswan High Dam on the Nile River. Nasser, in turn, used the termination of aid as justification to nationalize the Suez Canal. He described the takeover as an affirmation of Arab nationalism and anti-Zionism, declaring a ban on Israeli traffic through the canal. The initiative won widespread approval in Arab world; Western powers immediately condemned Nasser's actions.

Gamal Abdel Nasser played a central role in the Egyptian Revolution of 1952 and served as Egypt's president from 1956 until his death in 1970. His leadership inspired anticolonial revolutions during the Arab Nationalist Movement, and he founded groups such as the Palestine Liberation Organization in 1964.

A French sergeant distributes grenades to soldiers as they prepare to invade the Suez Canal after it was nationalized by Eyptian President Nasser on July 26, 1956.

PRELUDE TO INVASION

Over the course of the next several months, Egypt and the West held a series of negotiations to settle the issues that arose from the transfer. At the same time, British, French, and Israeli military planners began secret preparations to retake control of the canal. In the United States, the administration of Dwight D. Eisenhower did not want the crisis to escalate and sought a peaceful resolution. The British and the French, on the other hand, perceived the crisis as an opportunity to reassert influence and undermine Nasser's leadership of the Arab nationalist movement. A successful military intervention would have affirmed British authority in the region, halted Egyptian support to Algerian rebels fighting the French, and removed the significant adversary of Israel.

The Anglo-French-Israeli plan called for an Israeli invasion through the Sinai Desert. The British and French would then call for an immediate cessation of hostilities and invoke their right to protect the Suez Canal under the Tripartite Agreement of 1950. Upon the refusal of Egypt to withdraw, the Europeans would then take the canal by force. The British, French, and Israelis believed their actions would cause the collapse of the Nasser government.

OPENING SHOTS AND CONDEMNATION

On October 29, 1956, Israel invaded the Sinai Peninsula; Britain and France delivered an ultimatum to Nasser to turn over the canal on October 30. When the Egyptian leader failed to respond, the British and French initiated air strikes and used airborne troops to take control of the canal. The international community was outraged by their actions. In particular, President Eisenhower was furious over the way the British and French had talked peace while planning war and the fact that U.S. preferences were not heeded by the nation's closest allies.

Both the United States and the Soviet Union strongly rejected the British, French, and Israeli moves and demanded an immediate end to hostilities. The Eisenhower administration threatened to end oil shipments to Europe, where the economy was weak. It refused to provide economic aid to Britain, which was undergoing problems with its currency—the British pound—and France, which required World Bank loans to support its energy purchases. At the same time, the United States called on the United Nations to reinforce pressure for a political solution to the Israeli invasion. The U.S. government rebuffed thinly veiled Soviet threats to use force in support of the Egyptians as well

Prisoners taken by British and French forces were gathered at Port Fouad, across from Port Said in the Suez Canal. A number of men were taken prisoner within the first days of the Anglo-French intervention.

IMPLICATIONS

The Suez Crisis of 1956 ended with the waterway fully in Egyptian control and a great deal of Arab support throughout the Middle East for Nasser. His status as the leader of Arab nationalism was complete. In addition, the event pushed Egypt firmly into the Soviet sphere of influence for the next two decades of the cold war. By 1958, Egypt had secured Soviet assistance in completing the Aswan High Dam project. It also had signed military and technical assistance treaties. Nevertheless, Arab nationalism reached its peak in the immediate aftermath of the crisis. Further efforts by Nasser and others to form a Pan-Arab union meet with stiff resistance from other Arab leaders, despite the short-lived United Arab Republic (1958–1961) between Egypt and Syria.

The Suez Canal Crisis also marked the end of British and French primacy in the region. In July 1958, a revolution in Iraq overthrew the pro-British government, and in 1962, French forces withdrew from Algeria following its independence. Over the next decade, most of the remaining foreign colonies in Africa colonies declared their independence. The crisis also forced the United States to embrace its role as a world power, supplanting France and Great Britain.

Matt Williams and Jack Covarrubias

as a Soviet request for a joint Soviet-U.S. military solution to the crisis. Eisenhower feared that the Soviets would use the crisis to forge a bigger presence in the Middle East. U.S. efforts proved successful, and the British and French withdrew by December 22, 1956. Israel, facing less vulnerability to U.S. pressure, did not withdraw until March 7, 1957.

EISENHOWER AND U.S. POLICY IN THE SUEZ CRISIS

On October 31, 1956, President Eisenhower addressed the American people on the Hungarian Uprising and the Suez Crisis. Rejecting the use of force in either crisis, the president declared:

"In all the recent troubles in the Middle East, there have indeed been injustices suffered by all nations involved. But I do not believe that another instrument of injustice—war—is the remedy for these wrongs.
There can be no peace—without law. And there can be no law—if we were to invoke one code of international conduct for those who oppose us—and another for our friends.
The society of nations has been slow in developing means to apply this truth.
But the passionate longing for peace—on the part of all peoples of the earth compels us to speed our search for new and more effective instruments of justice.
The peace we seek and need means much more than mere absence of war. It means the acceptance of law, and the fostering of justice, in all the world."

GUIDED READING

Choueiri, Youssef M. *Arab Nationalism—A History: Nation and State in the Arab World.* Malden, MA: Blackwell Publishing, 2000.

Dawisha, A.I. *Arab Nationalism in the Twentieth Century: From Triumph to Despair.* Princeton, NJ: Princeton University Press, 2003.

Heikal, Mohamed H. *Cutting the Lion's Tail: Suez Through Egyptian Eyes.* New York: Arbor House, 1987.

Karabell, Zachary. *Parting the Desert: The Creation of the Suez Canal.* New York: Alfred A. Knopf, 2003.

THE SPACE RACE

The Space Race began as a competition between the United States and the Soviet Union for military superiority, but resulted in numerous technological benefits that transformed global commerce, medicine, and communications.

The race between the United States and the Soviet Union to explore space grew out of and worked in tandem with the arms race between the two superpowers. A critical element of space exploration was the development of rocket and missile technology, which was key to the interests of each nation in demonstrating military superiority over the other.

THE RACE BEGINS

The impetus for the space race occurred during World War II, with the invention of the atomic bomb in the United States and the development of rocket technology by German and Soviet scientists. In 1946, with the assistance of German rocket scientist Wernher von Braun (1912–1977), the developer of the V-2 rocket, the United States began its own missile-development program. Braun and other German scientists working for the U.S. government built upon the successes of the V-2—which in the early 1940s could climb to the upper reaches of the Earth's atmosphere—to develop rockets capable of carrying weapons over long distances and launching payloads into space for research and espionage purposes.

The early U.S. space program achieved several notable successes in the late 1940s and early 1950s, producing the first photographs of the Earth from space and conducting the first studies of the effects of space on animals by launching fruit flies, mice, and monkeys into suborbital flight.

RESPONSE TO SPUTNIK

Notions of American technological superiority were shattered with the launch of the first intercontinental ballistic missile by the Soviet Union in August 1957 and then by the launch of the first orbital satellite, *Sputnik I*, in early October 1957. *Sputnik* was a small, metal sphere capable only of transmitting a steady beeping tone, but its implications of Soviet technological superior-

ity and military advantage provoked a dramatic reaction from the United States. The American education system was revamped to place increased emphasis on mathematics and science, and on July 29, 1958, U.S. President Dwight D. Eisenhower signed legislation creating the National Aeronautics and Space Administration (NASA), a new federal agency responsible for creating a comprehensive national program of space exploration and travel. Besides assuming the responsibilities of the U.S. Army space program, which had launched the first American satellite, *Explorer I*, in January 1958, NASA would also focus much of its research on human space flight. Critical to this goal was the assembly of a crew of space travelers, called astronauts, to carry out research. The first teams of astronauts were chosen in 1959 from the ranks of military test pilots through extensive physical, medical, and psychological tests.

While the United States enjoyed a competitive advantage in satellite technology during the

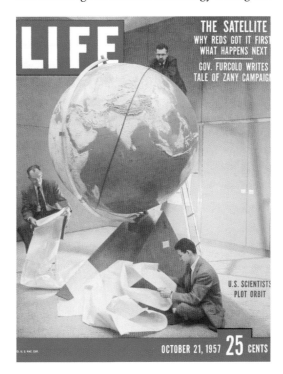

This *Life* magazine cover from 1957 shows scientists working at MIT in Cambridge, Massachusetts, as they calculate *Sputnik*'s orbit.

John Glenn was photographed in a spacesuit in February 1962, the month of his historic space flight.

late 1950s and early 1960s by launching the first weather and communications satellites, as well as several successful reconnaissance satellites, the Soviet Union took an early lead both in the advancement of human space flight and in the exploration of the moon. On April 12, 1961, Soviet "cosmonaut" Yuri Gagarin (1934–1968) became the first human in space, orbiting Earth for 108 minutes. The United States would launch astronaut Alan Shepard (1923–1998) into space less than one month later. Then in February 1962, astronaut John Glenn (1921–) became the first American in orbit, circling the Earth three times.

THE APOLLO PROGRAM

Despite American triumphs in the early space race, the moral victory that the Soviet Union had achieved by sending Gagarin into orbit, combined with other Soviet successes, fueled American fears of losing the space race. The U.S. government responded to these fears by launching the Apollo program, which had the primary mission of human exploration of the moon. Introducing the program to the American public in the early 1960s, President John F. Kennedy called upon NASA to land an astronaut on the moon before the end of the decade.

The U.S. effort to reach the moon first would proceed with widespread public support

and unprecedented government spending. Consisting of 15 manned missions (and several more unmanned missions), the Apollo program cost more than $25 million and employed more than 400,000 people, providing economic stimulus to the U.S. economy in general and to several states, most notably Florida and Texas.

Meanwhile, Soviet advances in space exploration continued throughout the early and mid-1960s. In 1963, the Soviet Union launched the first woman, Valentina Tereshkova, into space, and in subsequent years conducted the first mission with multiple crew members and the first spacewalk.

The centralized organization of NASA and its singular goal of achieving a moon landing gave the U.S. space program an advantage over that of the Soviet Union, where the aims of program leaders were often divergent and dependent upon the patronage of political leaders for fulfillment. Soviet Premier Nikita Khrushchev had responded to Kennedy's pledge to place Americans on the moon by the end of the 1960s, stating that the Soviet Union had no plans for such a mission. Yet chief Soviet scientists insisted that a moon mission was within reach, and the Soviets continued to explore the moon in unmanned flights, circling it with a satellite in 1966.

Plans for a manned moon mission by Soviet astronauts were well under way by the mid-1960s, but they were derailed by a series of accidents and mechanical failures. By 1969, Soviet plans had been placed on hold. Meanwhile, NASA's plans for a manned moon mission proceeded as planned, and on July 21, 1969, American astronaut Neil Armstrong (1930–), commander of the *Apollo 11* mission, became the first human to set foot on the moon, while an estimated 500 million people around the world watched via television broadcast.

JOINT INITIATIVE

By the mid-1970s, the priorities of both the United States and the Soviet Union had changed with regard to space exploration. Both nations had poured large amounts of money and national resources into their space programs, and the United States, having won the race to the moon that had largely driven the two programs throughout the 1960s, abandoned the Apollo program to concentrate on the development of

---

A PRESIDENT'S CHALLENGE

In a 1962 address at Rice University, U.S. President John F. Kennedy invoked nationalistic ideals of American ingenuity and competitive spirit in announcing a bold initiative to reach the moon before the end of the decade:

"We choose to go to the moon. We choose to go to the moon in this decade and do the other things, not only because they are easy, but because they are hard, because that goal will serve to organize and measure the best of our energies and skills, because that challenge is one that we are willing to accept, one we are unwilling to postpone, and one which we intend to win, and the others, too."

The fervid pace of the space race produced a rapid succession of achievements on the part of both superpowers, but was intermittently marred by fatal accidents. The largest such disaster occurred in 1960, when a Soviet rocket exploded on the launchpad, killing dozens of personnel. Another fatal mission occurred on January 27, 1967, when U.S. astronauts Virgil "Gus" Grissom (1926–1967), Ed White (1930–1967), and Roger Chafee (1935–1967) died in a launchpad fire while preparing to embark on an *Apollo 1* mission. In April 1967, a *Soyuz I* voyage ended in tragedy when the spacecraft, carrying Soviet astronaut Vladimir Komarov (1927–1967), crashed upon reentry. Three other Soviet astronauts perished in 1971 during the reentry of a *Soyuz 11* spacecraft. Several Soviet cosmonauts also were killed in related missions, most notably the first man in space, Gagarin, who died in a fighter-jet crash in 1968.

space stations and reusable space shuttles. The Soviet Union followed suit and, after *Apollo-Soyuz*—a joint mission by the two superpowers in 1975—both countries shifted the focus of the space race to cooperative international ventures emphasizing scientific research.

Despite its origins as an adjunct to the cold war, the space race produced a plethora of technological innovations and scientific discoveries, contributing substantially to the advancement of world commerce, health care, communications, meteorology, and astronomy. Decades of information gathered from space missions has dramatically expanded scientific knowledge of Earth's upper atmosphere, the surface of the moon, the solar system, and the universe as a whole.

Technological advances came at the expense of large amounts of money and national resources. Expenditures of the Soviet Union's space program, estimated to have peaked at between $4 billion and $7 billion per year, have

Astronaut Thomas Stafford and Cosmonaut Alexei Leonov were pictured on the Apollo-Soyuz mission in 1975.

been cited as a contributor to the eventual economic collapse of the Soviet Union in the early 1990s.

Michael H. Burchett

Technology developed as a result of the space race can be found in virtually every aspect of modern life. The following is a small sampling of the numerous innovations produced by the space program research:

Household: freeze-dried foods, smoke detectors, cordless power tools, ionizing water purifiers, light-emitting diodes (LEDs)

Health care: Magnetic Resonance Imaging (MRI), digital mammography, lifelike artificial limbs

Sports: waterproof dome roofs, helmets, shin guards

Communications: Global Positioning Systems (GPS), satellite dish service, virtual reality

GUIDED READING

Cadbury, Deborah. *Space Race: The Epic Battle Between America and the Soviet Union for Dominion of Space.* New York: HarperCollins, 2006.

Siddiqi, Asif A. *Sputnik and the Soviet Space Challenge.* Gainesville: University Press of Florida, 2003.

Stott, Carole. *Space Exploration.* New York: Alfred A. Knopf, 1997.

THE NEW FRONTIER AND ALLIANCE FOR PROGRESS

In proclaiming a new era of governmental activism in both domestic and foreign policy, U.S. President John F. Kennedy introduced the Alliance for Progress in 1961. The cooperative venture involved the United States and 22 other nations and was designed to promote economic and social development in Latin America. The alliance achieved mixed results throughout the 1960s and was disbanded in the early 1970s.

In his acceptance speech to the Democratic National Convention in 1960, presidential candidate John F. Kennedy declared that the United States faced a "new frontier" of foreign and domestic challenges, and he called for massive mobilization of public and private resources to address these challenges. Upon his election to the presidency, Kennedy adopted the "New Frontier" theme as a moniker for his ambitious array of social and economic development programs, which included an activist foreign policy focused on containing the spread of communism around the world, particularly in the Western Hemisphere. Communist revolution in Cuba in the late 1950s fueled fears that communism would spread to other countries in Central and South America, many of which were mired in poverty and torn by civil strife.

ORGANIZATION AND OBJECTIVES

For many years, the U.S. government had provided economic aid to individual Latin American countries, yet no coordinated effort to aid the region as a whole had ever been implemented. In 1961, in order to quell the influence of Communist ideology in Latin America, Kennedy proposed a cooperative effort between the United States and Latin American nations to promote economic development, strengthen health and education programs, and facilitate democratic government. The collaboration, dubbed The Alliance for Progress, officially began on August 17, 1961, when representatives of 19 Latin American countries met in Punta del Este, Uruguay, to sign a charter. Three additional Latin American counties later would join the program.

COMMONALITY VS. COMMUNISM

In a 1961 address at a White House reception for the Diplomatic Corps of the Latin American Republics, President John F. Kennedy invoked the New Frontier theme to promote pan-Americanism and discourage Central and South American nations from embracing revolutionary ideology:

"The genius of our scientists has given us the tools to bring abundance to our land, strength to our industry, and knowledge to our people. For the first time we have the capacity to strike off the remaining bonds of poverty and ignorance—to free our people for the spiritual and intellectual fulfillment which has always been the goal of our civilization.

Yet at this very moment of maximum opportunity, we confront the same forces which have imperiled America throughout its history—the alien forces which once again seek to impose the despotisms of the Old World on the people of the New. ...

Our continents are bound together by a common history, the endless exploration of new frontiers. Our nations are the product of a common struggle, the revolt from colonial rule. And our people share a common heritage, the quest for the dignity and the freedom of man."

Hacia la 'Alianza para el Progreso'

Por JOHN F. KENNEDY

El Presidente de los Estados Unidos
define la meta común de las Américas
en los turbulentos años de esta época

El ansia de progreso que hoy inflama el espíritu de los hombres de todo este hemisferio señala tan sólo la etapa más reciente de la eterna revolución de las Américas. La República de los Estados Unidos del Norte fue creada por Washington y Jefferson antes de que la democracia llegase a Europa. Bolívar y San Martín alcanzaron la independencia de países de Sudamérica antes de que se derrumbaran los sistemas coloniales de ultramar. La revolución social era ya realidad en México antes de que Rusia sacudiera el feudalismo zarista. Y en casi todos los aspectos del progreso nacional, la América del Norte y la del Sur han marcado el rumbo hacia una sociedad más fecunda y más libre.

Hoy las naciones de América enfrentan un nuevo reto en su calidad de guías. Los milagros de la ciencia moderna han acercado el día en que toda la humanidad podrá vivir con decencia a salvo de la degradación de la miseria, la ignorancia y el hambre—libre para la conquista de la satisfacción que proporcionan las metas intelectuales y espirituales logradas. Ese era el sueño de Martí cuando batallaba por la independencia de Cuba.

Ese es el sueño que mi país—agraciado con abundantes recursos naturales—ha demostrado que está a nuestro alcance. Y ése es el sueño que debe constituir nuestro objetivo común a lo largo de los turbulentos años de esta última mitad del siglo XX.

He prometido la vigorosa participación de los Estados Unidos en un esfuerzo común por realizar ese propósito, mediante la formación de una nueva "Alianza para el Progreso" entre todas las naciones del continente. Pero para triunfar, será preciso aunar las energías y la imaginación de todos los pueblos de América. Debemos trabajar en el desarrollo de nuevos recursos, en la reforma de sistemas de distribución agraria, en organizar mercados comunes, establecer fábricas, diversificar la producción agrícola, construir carreteras, hospitales y sistemas de abastecimiento de aguas de los cuales depende la continuidad del progreso, y lograr que todos los ciudadanos—obreros, campesinos, empleados y profesionales—compartan por igual el adelanto de las Américas.

Nosotros, en los Estados Unidos, no nos oponemos a los cambios sociales y económicos en las Américas. Al contrario, damos

la bienvenida a esa revolución pacífica, como clave de una futura fortaleza. Ni tampoco nos oponemos a ningún instrumento o institución que puedan forjarse para producir ese cambio, puesto que creemos que cada nación debe ser libre de escoger su propio camino hacia el progreso. Pero creemos también que el adelanto fructífero sólo es posible cuando los pueblos tienen libertad para labrar su propio destino, y que la Alianza para el Progreso triunfará sólo cuando toda forma de tiranía—ya sea el despotismo nacional o la dominación extranjera—haya sido desterrada del continente.

COMO primer paso en nuestra Nueva Alianza, he pedido al Congreso de los EE.UU. que provea 500 millones de dólares para dar comienzo al desarrollo metódico del continente. Al mismo tiempo, los EE.UU. enviarán a la América Latina una misión que determine procedimientos para utilizar nuestra abundancia de productos alimenticios a fin de aliviar el hambre. Y con objeto de que nunca se traten con negligencia las

necesidades de nuestros vecinos, he organizado un grupo especial para que coordine—en el más alto nivel—todos nuestros programas y planes concernientes a las naciones americanas.

Continuaremos haciendo lo que nos corresponde; y esperamos confiados los esfuerzos cada día mayores de todos los pueblos de América. Porque trabajando juntos y bajo el signo de la libertad, no hay objetivo ni ideal que nos esté vedado. Y juntos crearemos un continente en que el bienestar humano impere sin sacrificio de la libertad, en que todos los hombres tengan derecho a aspirar a una vida digna, y en que nuestros hijos puedan superar hasta nuestros sueños más optimistas.

"Necesitaremos—todos nosotros—la misma determinación, la misma consagración, para mantener el rumbo a lo largo de la gran era de exploración y de descubrimientos que nos espera."

Franklin Roosevelt dijo en 1944: "Recuerdo que cuando Colón iba a hacerse a la mar, en el verano de 1492, escribió al principio de su libro de bitácora estas palabras: 'Ante todo, es muy importante que me olvide de dormir, y que me dedique mucho a la navegación, porque eso es necesario.'

The goals of the Alliance for Progress included growing the economies of each member nation by at least 2.5 percent per year, eliminating illiteracy in the region by 1970, ensuring more equal distribution of land and income, and establishing democratic governments. Participants in the Alliance for Progress would provide 80 percent of the funding for its programs, totaling a proposed $80 billion over 10 years. The United States would provide an additional $20 billion during this period. A variety of international entities and U.S. government agencies were responsible for coordinating Alliance for Progress programs, including the Organization of American States, the World Bank, the Agency for International Development, the Import-Export Bank, and the Peace Corps.

MIXED RESULTS

The formation of the Alliance for Progress resulted in an immediate and dramatic increase in the amount of American aid flowing into Central and South American countries. The total amount of U.S. aid into Latin America in 1961 nearly tripled that of 1960. Alliance for Progress projects funded with this aid included the construction of housing developments, roads, bridges, and power plants, and the improvement of the educational systems of participating nations. The emphasis on developing education and infrastructure was crucial to achieving the goal of increasing the economic growth of member nations. The Alliance for Progress largely achieved this goal, as most member nations met or exceeded their target growth rates during the 1960s.

Communication was considered critical to the success of the Alliance for Progress, as evidenced by this Spanish translation of a newspaper article by John F. Kennedy.

U.S. Peace Corps volunteers, funded by the Alliance for Progress, are pictured working with children in Colombia.

Despite increasing overall economic growth in Latin America, the Alliance for Progress failed to reduce substantially the historically high rates of unemployment in member nations, primarily due to steadily increasing population rates in these nations. Improvements in education and healthcare, while significant, were also largely offset by population growth and the increased use of labor-saving machinery, a by-product of the industrial growth that the program itself had helped stimulate.

Direct efforts by the Alliance for Progress to quell the activities of revolutionary movements produced equally mixed results. From its inception, the Alliance for Progress provoked derision, suspicion, and resistance from both the left and the right of the political spectrum in Latin America. Wealthy business owners and large landowners opposed its social welfare programs and land reform efforts, while revolutionaries such as Ernesto "Che" Guevara (1928–1967) derided the Alliance for Progress as a vehicle of American imperialism and the advancement of American business interests in Central and South America.

During the administration of Lyndon B. Johnson, who succeeded Kennedy as president in 1963, an increased focus on military assistance to close U.S. allies in Latin America exacerbated political instability in the region. Factions on the left and right took advantage of anti-U.S. sentiment to rally forces. Some Latin American governments fell to military coups, at least one of which, in Brazil in 1964, was carried out with the approval of the U.S. government. By the end of the 1960s, several Latin American nations formerly under constitutional governments were ruled by military dictatorships.

FAILED INTERVENTION

The military campaign known as the Latin American Security Operation, whose objective was direct confrontation of Communist and Socialist organizations, organized an attack on a group of leftist rebels who had established a Socialist peasant enclave known as Marquetalia in Colombia during the 1950s. In May 1964, a force of about 16,000 Colombian troops, aided by U.S. military advisors, attacked the enclave with an air and ground assault that destroyed the compound and dispersed the peasant fighters. The fighters later reformed as the Revolutionary Armed Forces of Colombia (FARC), which would become one of the most powerful leftist paramilitary organizations in Latin America.

A GRIM ASSESSMENT

A committee chaired by Nelson Rockefeller (*left*) issued a scathing report on the Alliance for Progress in 1968.

Following the assassination of President John F. Kennedy in 1963, the commitment of his successors to the Alliance for Progress and its original goals wavered. President Lyndon B. Johnson was able to convince Congress to maintain U.S. financial commitments to the program, but he increasingly emphasized military force over civil reform. When Richard M. Nixon assumed the presidency in January 1969, he assigned low priority to the Alliance for Progress, appointing New York Governor Nelson Rockefeller, one of his chief rivals in the Republican Party, to visit Latin America and report on the success of Alliance for Progress programs.

During four visits to Latin American nations, Rockefeller was met with anti-American demonstrations and expressions of frustration over the failure of Latin American governments to enact needed reforms, particularly with regard to land redistribution. The Rockefeller Report concluded that economic aid had done little to fuel political reform, and that the $20 billion that the United States had committed to the alliance—less than $10 per citizen—had been insufficient to effect the transformation of the entire continent.

DECLINE AND AFTERMATH

Although the Alliance for Progress continued to operate through the early 1970s, its influence dwindled substantially in the late 1960s, when the U.S. government, under increasing financial strain from the Vietnam War, began cutting funding for aid to Latin America. The U.S. commitment to the Alliance for Progress was further reduced after a report for the White House by New York Governor Nelson Rockefeller (1908–1979) in 1969 concluded that the program had been largely ineffective in raising standards of living and discouraging the rise of revolutionary political groups.

In 1973, the Organization of American States officially ended the Alliance for Progress by disbanding the committee that oversaw it. Estimates of total funding provided by the United States during the life of the program vary according to the reported amount of return on loans and investments, ranging from $10 billion to more than $22 billion.

The demise of the Alliance for Progress signaled a shift in the focus of U.S. economic policy toward Latin America from one of financial aid to increased trade. The change ultimately led to the adoption of free-trade treaties such as the North American Free Trade Agreement (NAFTA) in 1994 and the Central American Free Trade Agreement (CAFTA) in 2005.

Michael H. Burchett

GUIDED READING

Guevara, Ernesto. *Our America and Theirs: Kennedy and the Alliance for Progress.* New York: Ocean Press, 2006.

Lowenthal, Abraham F., ed. *Exporting Democracy: The United States and Latin America.* Baltimore: Johns Hopkins University Press, 1991.

Scheman, Ronald L. *The Alliance for Progress: A Retrospective.* New York: Praeger, 1988.

Smith, Peter H. *Talons of the Eagle: Dynamics of U.S.-Latin American Relations.* New York: Oxford University Press, 2000.

Taffet, Jeffrey F. *Foreign Aid as Foreign Policy: The Alliance for Progress in Latin America.* New York: Routledge, 2007.

THE CUBAN MISSILE CRISIS

The 1962 Cuban Missile Crisis was the result of the discovery of Soviet nuclear missiles in Cuba, an ally of the Soviet Union. During a period of 13 days, the world remained on the brink of nuclear conflict, but U.S. President John F. Kennedy crafted a compromise to avert war.

MISSILE TRANSPORTERS

12 PROB GUIDELINE MISSILES

HEAVY EQUIPMENT

5 MISSILE DOLLIES

20' LONG CYLINDRICAL TANKS

MISSILE TRANSPORTERS

OPEN STORAGE

It was clear to American officials that nuclear missiles were located in Cuba. This photo dated October 24, 1962, shows missiles, as well as related nuclear equipment and transportation.

In 1959, Cuban revolutionary Fidel Castro overthrew the pro-American Cuban dictator Fulgencio Batista (1901–1973) and initiated economic and political relations with the Soviet Union. After the United States launched the 1961 Bay of Pigs invasion, a failed effort to overthrow Castro, the Cuban leader created a stronger alliance with the Soviet Union. Cuba began receiving Soviet economic and military aid, prompting the Kennedy administration to enact economic sanctions against the island nation. Castro and other Cuban leaders became increasingly convinced that the United States was planning to invade Cuba, an illusion partially facilitated by Soviet intelligence. In response, Castro appealed to the Soviets for greater assistance, and in April 1962, Moscow deployed coastal defense cruise missiles and several thousand troops to Cuba. The Soviets also offered in May to station nuclear missiles in Cuba, ostensibly as a deterrent against invasion, but also to offset U.S. advantages created by the deployment of American nuclear missiles to allied countries such as Turkey, which bordered the Soviet Union.

MISSILES IN CUBA AND THE U.S. RESPONSE

In July 1962, American spy planes began to view increased military activity in Cuba. On August 29, new air defense missile sites were spotted. One month later, American intelligence officials confirmed that medium-range ballistic missiles were being transported to the island nation from the Soviet Union. On October 15, a U.S. reconnaissance airplane captured pictures of Soviet SS-4 nuclear missiles in Cuba. The following day, Kennedy administration officials began discussing options, including an aerial campaign to destroy the missile sites, an invasion of Cuba, and a negotiated settlement. Over the next several days, U.S. intelligence identified three nuclear missile sites under construction. On October 18, Kennedy met with the Soviet for-

eign minister, who vehemently denied that any missile sites were being built.

On October 21, Kennedy decided to impose a naval "quarantine," or blockade, around Cuba as a first step. The next day, President Kennedy conducted a televised address to the American people, in which he informed them of the missile installations and his decision to initiate the blockade. The following day, the Organization of American States voted to endorse the U.S. blockade.

After Kennedy's speech, Soviet Premier Nikita Khrushchev (1894–1971) sent a telegram to President Kennedy advising that the missiles were simply a deterrent against American missiles in Turkey. Khrushchev stated the Soviet Union had peaceful intentions and the missiles would not be used against the United States unless American forces perpetrated an attack first. He also denounced the idea of a naval blockade. Soviet ships reached the quarantine line on October 24, but Khrushchev ordered

CHRONOLOGY

1962

August 29 An American U-2 spy plane photographs military sites being constructed in Cuba.

October 14 U-2 spy plane photographs the presence of missile sites in Cuba.

October 22 President Kennedy addresses the nation, stating the discovery of nuclear missiles in Cuba.

October 23 Nikita Khrushchev writes a telegram to President Kennedy stating the deterrent purpose of the missiles.

October 24 The American naval blockade of Cuba takes effect.

October 27 An American U-2 spy plane is shot down over Cuba.

October 28 The Soviet Union agrees to dismantle the nuclear missile sites in Cuba.

November 20 The United States ends its quarantine of Cuba.

As the world sat on the edge of nuclear war, President Kennedy signed a proclamation for a Cuban naval quarantine on October 23, 1962.

them to stop and not to provoke the American vessels. The next day, the United States confronted the Soviets at the United Nations with their photographic evidence. The incident was part of a larger public-relations campaign on the part of the United States to rally world opinion in its favor.

On October 26, Kennedy received another message from Khrushchev, stating that the Soviets would dismantle the weapons if the United States promised not to invade Cuba and ended its blockade. On October 25 and 26, a number of ships entering Cuba were searched, and after inspection, were allowed to pass through. On October 27, tensions rose further as an American U-2 spy plane, a high-altitude, reconnaissance aircraft, was shot down over Cuba while taking photographs of the military installations. That day, Kennedy received another telegram from Khrushchev, which added the demand that America withdraw its missiles from Turkey as another condition for the Soviet withdrawal. The president chose to ignore the telegram and instead accepted the Soviet pre-

NIKITA KHRUSHCHEV (1894–1971)

Nikita Khrushchev (pictured to the right, next to Fidel Castro) served as the Soviet premier from 1958 through 1964. Khrushchev rapidly rose through the Communist Party during the 1930s and 1940s. After Stalin's death in 1953, Khrushchev emerged as the leader of the Soviet Union. He launched a series of reforms and denounced the excesses of his predecessor, Josef Stalin. Khruschchev was named Soviet premier in 1958. He faced significant criticism within the leadership of the Communist Party for his management of the Cuban Missile Crisis. Many Soviet officials believed that Khrushchev's actions made the Soviet Union look weak and unable to stand up to the United States. Khrushchev was forced from office in 1964.

DISMANTLING THE MISSILES

Nikita Khrushchev's message to John F. Kennedy on October 28, 1962, was delivered in Russian on Moscow Radio. In it, he announced the dismantling of nuclear missile bases in Cuba:

"I received your message of 27 October and I am grateful for your appreciation of the responsibility you bear for world peace and security. The Soviet government has ordered the dismantling of bases and the dispatch of equipment to the U.S.S.R. A few days ago, Havana was shelled, allegedly by Cuban émigrés. Yet someone must have armed them for this purpose. Even a British cargo ship was shelled. Cubans want to be masters of their country. The threat of invasion has upset the Cuban people. I wish to again state that the Soviet government has offered Cuba only defensive weapons. I appreciate your assurance that the United States will not invade Cuba. Hence, we have ordered our officers to stop building bases, dismantle the equipment, and send it back home. This can be done under UN supervision. We must not allow the situation to deteriorate, (but) eliminate hotbeds of tension, and we must see to it that no other conflicts occur which might lead to a world nuclear war. We are ready to continue to exchange views on relations between NATO and the Warsaw Bloc, disarmament, and other issues of peace and war."

mier's earlier proposal to withdraw the missiles and bombers in exchange for an end to the blockade and a U.S. pledge not to invade Cuba. Turkey indicated its desire to retain the missiles as a deterrent against the Soviet Union and Kennedy did not want to alienate America's NATO ally. He pledged to secretly withdraw the U.S. missiles to avoid causing any public embarrassment to the Turkish government.

DISASTER AVERTED

On October 28, the Soviets agreed to dismantle the missile operations in Cuba with the assistance and verification of the United Nations. UN officials worked with Fidel Castro to verify the dismantlement of the missile sites. On November 20, the United States ended its blockade of Cuba.

The nuclear missiles were eventually returned to the Soviet Union and the United States secretly dismantled their own missile sites in Turkey three months later. In the years that followed, the relationship between the United States and the Soviet Union was strengthened. A "hotline" was created between the two nations in order to keep all lines of communication open in order to prevent a nuclear disaster and to limit military escalations.

In 1963, the Limited Nuclear Test Ban Treaty was signed between the United States, the Soviet Union, and the United Kingdom. This treaty recognized the harmful effects of nuclear testing and banned nuclear testing in the atmosphere, in outer space, and underwater. The superpowers initiated new negotiations to limit their nuclear weapons.

Gavin Wilk

GUIDED READING

Beschloss, Michael R. *The Crisis Years: Kennedy and Khrushchev, 1960–1963.* New York: Edward Burlingame Books, 1991.

Blight, James G. *On the Brink: Americans and Soviets Reexamine the Cuban Missile Crisis.* New York: Hill and Wang, 1989.

Frankel, Max. *High Noon in the Cold War: Kennedy, Khrushchev, and the Cuban Missile Crisis.* New York: Ballantine Books, 2004.

John F. Kennedy Presidential Library. http://www.jfklibrary.org.

Polmar, Norman, and John D. Gresham. *Defcon 2: Standing on the Brink of Nuclear War During the Cuban Missile Crisis.* Hoboken, NJ: Wiley, 2006.

LIST OF ILLUSTRATIONS

GLOSSARY

Allied Powers Combined forces of Great Britain, France, Russia, and the United States during the two world wars

Allied Supreme War Council Group of Allied representatives that coordinated military strategy from 1917 through the end of World War I

Anglo-American Term referring to Great Britain and the United States and their mutual security interests during and after World War II

Anglo-Iranian Oil Company (AIOC) British-led oil company created in 1933 that drilled in Iran and shared its profits with the Iranian government; the company was nationalized by Iran in 1951

apartheid System most commonly associated with South Africa from 1948 through 1994, when nonwhite South Africans faced repression and unequal rights under a national system of racial law

appeasement Tactic of granting concessions to potential enemies in order to maintain peace and stability; the policy of appeasement was adopted by British Prime Minister Neville Chamberlain in his dealings with Adolf Hitler, including allowing Germany to occupy the Sudetenland in Czechoslovakia in 1938

Aswan High Dam Geographically important dam for sustained economic development; U.S. and British withdrawal of funds in 1956 to support the maintenance of the facility sparked Egyptian President Nasser's nationalization of the Suez Canal

Axis Powers The countries of Germany, Italy, and Japan engaged against the Allied nations in World War II

banana republic Any of the small countries in the tropics, especially in the Western Hemisphere, whose economies are largely dependent on fruit exports, tourism, and foreign investment

blitzkrieg German word meaning "lightning war," a military tactic used by Nazi armed forces during World War II to create shock with extreme firepower

British Commonwealth Association of sovereign states consisting of the United Kingdom and a number of its former dependencies and colonies

Central American Free Trade Agreement (CAFTA) A free-trade agreement among Costa Rica, the Dominican Republic, El Salvador, Guatemala, Honduras, Nicaragua, and the United States that was ratified in its final form in 2004

Central Powers The World War I alliance of Germany, Austria-Hungary, Turkey, and Bulgaria

Chinese Exclusion Act Federal law passed on May 6, 1882, that banned immigration from China

cold war Period of tension between the United States and Soviet Union that began after World War II and lasted until the collapse of the Soviet Union in 1991

Committee on Government Operations U.S. Senate committee established in 1946 to serve as a watchdog for the federal government

contract laborers Workers hired in one country and brought to another, usually in groups, to work for a fixed period of time in return for a fixed wage as well as transportation, housing, food, and medical care

Cuban Revolution Uprising in Cuba during which the dictatorship of Fulgencio Batista (1952–1959) was overthrown and the government of revolutionary leader Fidel Castro was brought to power

dollar diplomacy Method of furthering foreign policy aims and extending U.S. power through the guarantee of loans to foreign countries used by President Taft in the early 1900s

eastern front The area of fighting in World War I that occurred primarily in central and eastern Europe from the Baltic Sea southward

Emergency Quota Act Law passed in 1921 that limited the number of immigrants based on the number of people of certain nationalities already in the United States

European Union Federation of European member nations in the post–World War II era dedicated to closer economic and political cooperation

executive order A rule or regulation issued by the U.S. president that does not need approval from Congress

Fourteen Points A list of objectives formulated by President Woodrow Wilson and his foreign policy advisors in early 1918 in anticipation of the end of World War I; among these objectives was the formation of a League of Nations to promote world peace.

French–Algerian War War from 1954 until 1962 that resulted in Algeria winning its independence from France

Good Neighbor policy Policy of President Franklin D. Roosevelt relating to Latin America and Europe from 1933 through 1945 that renounced unpopular military intervention and promoted friendly methods of influence

great power Term used to refer to the world's most powerful nations

gross national product Total value of goods and services produced in a given nation during a given period of time

Hindenburg Line The first line of German defense constructed from 1916 to 1917 that ran from the Belgian North Sea coast south toward Rheims, France, and through Verdun, France

Holocaust Genocidal program of the Nazis against the Jews in Europe in the 1930s and 1940s that killed an estimated 6 million people

House Un-American Activities Committee (HUAC) A special committee established in 1938 by the House of Representatives to investigate disloyalty and organizations it deemed subversive or disloyal

imperial rescript Decree issued by a country's supreme authority

interventionism Intervening in another country's affairs

iron curtain Term coined by British Prime Minister Winston Churchill to describe the imaginary line that divided Communist and non-Communist Europe after World War II

irreconcilables A group of 14 Senate Republicans who, during the 1919 debate over the Treaty of Versailles, opposed U.S. participation in the League of Nations

League of Nations International organization authorized by the Treaty of Versailles (1919) to promote world peace and cooperation

Lend-Lease Act U.S. law passed in March 1941 that appropriated money for the lending or leasing of arms and other supplies to non-Axis countries

mandate Area granted by the League of Nations for administration to help prepare for independence

Manhattan Project Project established in 1942 under the Army Corps of Engineers to develop an atomic bomb

Meiji Restoration Political revolution in Japan during the late nineteenth century that resulted in the industrialization of Japan, which came into competition with the leading imperial powers of the period

Monroe Doctrine Doctrine issued by President James Monroe in 1823, which stated that European nations were to no longer interfere in the affairs of newly independent nations or create colonies in the Western Hemisphere

National Origins Act Part of the Immigration Act of 1924 that limited the number of U.S. immigrants who could be admitted from any country to 2 percent of the number of people from that country already in the United States

New Deal Set of Great Depression programs designed to give relief to the poor, reform the banking system, and bring recovery to the economy

nonviolent civil disobedience Form of protest pioneered by Mohandas K. Gandhi during the Indian independence movement; Gandhi's successful use of nonviolent civil disobedience inspired other protest movements, most notably Martin Luther King, Jr., and the civil rights movement

North American Free Trade Agreement (NAFTA) A free-trade agreement between Canada, Mexico, and the United States ratified in 1994 that lowers tariffs and promotes trade and investment between the three countries

North Atlantic Treaty Organization (NATO) A mutual defense alliance created in 1949, comprising 26 North American and European member nations as of 2008

Open Door policy Policy created by American Secretary of State John Hay in 1899 that focused on the creation of equal trade throughout China

Organization of American States A regional organization created in 1948 to promote the economic and social development of Latin America

Pan-Africanism Political and cultural philosophy that emphasizes the solidarity of all peoples of African descent across the world

Panama Canal Human-made canal opened in 1914 that joined the Atlantic and Pacific Oceans, reducing travel time from one ocean to the other almost in half

People's Republic of China Communist government of mainland China created in 1949

pogrom Riot directed at ethnic and religious groups, in particular to destroy their property

Qing Dynasty Ruling dynasty of China from 1644 until 1911

reparations Compensation in money or materials payable by a defeated nation for damages to or expenditures sustained by another nation as a result of hostilities with the defeated nation

reprisal Act of retaliation

resolution Formal statement that specifies a decided course of action, which is adopted and followed by a governing body

Roosevelt Corollary Amendment to the Monroe Doctrine made by President Theodore Roosevelt in 1904 that argued that the United States was justified in intervening in Caribbean nations if they were unable to pay their international debts

Security Council Permanent body of the United Nations consisting of 15 member nations focused on maintaining peace and security throughout the world

Smith Act U.S. federal law passed in 1940 making it illegal to advocate the overthrow of the government or to belong to an organization supporting such overthrow

sphere of influence Country or region under the influence of an external power

Suez Canal Company The regulatory body for the Suez Canal established in 1858 by the Spanish engineer Ferdinand de Lesseps

thirty-eighth parallel Line of latitude that divides North and South Korea; a demilitarization zone currently exists along this line

Treaty of Brest Litovsk Treaty signed in March 1918 between the Central Powers and Russia, under which Russia lost more than 300,000 square miles (775,000 square kilometers) of territory, including the areas of Latvia, Estonia, and Lithuania

Treaty of Versailles The peace treaty signed on June 28, 1919, that officially ended World War I

Tripartite Pact Military alliance signed by Germany, Italy, and Japan during World War II

Triple Entente The World War I alliance of Russia, Britain, and France

Truman Doctrine Doctrine that promised American support for "free peoples" facing internal or external subversion, thus signaling an expansive American commitment to opposing the advance of communism worldwide

trusteeship Territory administered by the United Nations to help prepare for independence

United Arab Republic Political union between 1958 and 1961 of Egypt and Syria. This was also the official name of Egypt until 1971.

United Fruit Company Company formed in 1899 in Costa Rica by two Americans that spread across Central America and dominated the fruit industry by the 1960s

United Nations International organization created in 1945 dedicated to the peaceful resolution of conflicts between nations

western front Main theater of war in western Europe during World War I in which British, French, and American forces fought the German army along an unbroken line stretching from the English Channel through southern Belgium and across northern France to the Swiss border

yellow fever Viral disease transmitted to humans by mosquitoes, so-named as one of its symptoms is jaundice

yellow journalism Form of journalism that utilizes sensational headlines and images to increase readership

Zionism Movement to restore Palestine as the homeland of the Jewish people

INDEX

In this index, bold indicates a glossary term, m represents a map, p represents a photograph or illustration, and c represents a chronology.